AF647632

THE COMPLETE PRIVATE INVESTIGATOR'S GUIDE BOOK

CDR SUNIL SRIVASTAVA, (RETD.)

BlueRose Publishers

© Sunil Srivastava 2021

All rights reserved

All rights reserved by author. No part of this publication may be reproduced, stored in a retrieval system or transmitted in any form or by any means, electronic, mechanical, photocopying, recording or otherwise, without the prior written permission of the author.

Although every precaution has been taken to verify the accuracy of the information contained herein, the author and publisher assume no responsibility for any errors or omissions. No liability is assumed for damages that may result from the use of information contained within.

First Published in June 2021

ISBN: 978-93-5427-941-6

BLUEROSE PUBLISHERS

www.bluerosepublishers.com

info@bluerosepublishers.com

+91 8882 898 898

Cover Design:

Mohammad Fayez Zameer

Typographic Design:

Ilma Mirza

Distributed by: BlueRose, Amazon, Flipkart

This book will herald a new era of the Detective Profession

Abbreviations Used in this Book

PI	Private Investigator
IT	Information Technology
CDR	Call Data Records
SDR	Subscriber Data Records
IS	Information Security
FIR	First Information Report
ISP	Internet Service Provider
DUI	Driving Under Influence
PT	Pending Trial
UD	UnDetected
SHO	Station House Officer (In-charge of Police Station)
UI	Under Investigation
IPC	Indian Penal Code
IO	Investigating Officer
Cr.P.C	Criminal Procedure Code
IEA	Indian Evidence Act

POLICE RANK STRUCTURE

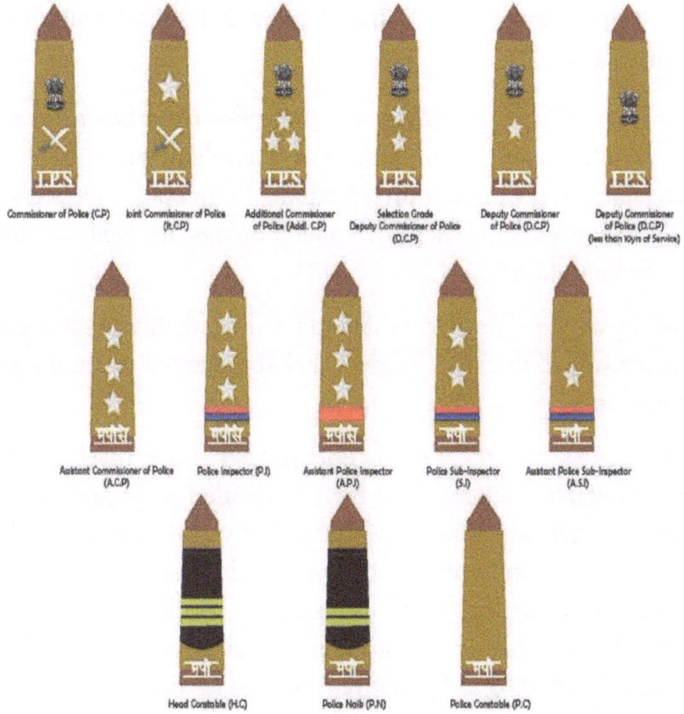

Preface

Whether or not you have earned yourself a decent education in psychology, medical science, marketing, technical or journalism, find yourself welcomed here. If you find yourself intrigued in the shenanigans of silent revelations of others' activities, this book is tailored for you!

While designing the Diploma in Comprehensive Cyber Investigation Course comprising modules like Cyber Security, Ethical Hacking, Cyber Forensics and Practical Investigation, for Cyber Crime Helpline LLP, it dawned on me that such practical skills and knowledge can benefit to empower the Private Investigator and subsequently boost the job prospects as well.

"The complete Private Investigator's guide Book" is based on how one can do Private Investigation and is a complete guide book on the technology based fact finding investigations. The book covers all aspects of handling conventional detective methodology as well as the cyber detective methodology.

Any student of the detective profession will find this book a complete guide comprising of the knowledge and skills essential to handle any type of investigation.

The book guides one on how to undertake Private Investigation both digitally and conventionally. The book is divided in 4 parts viz. Part 1 to 4. Part 1 covers how to improve oneself in various aspects – Power of observation & concentration, communicating skills, writing skills, perseverance & patience, quick thinking & discretion, memory, note taking, etc. Part 2 covers preparation, working methodology, types of investigations undertaken by conventional detective agencies. Part 3 brings out the techniques of digital investigation which when compounded with the conventional investigation methodologies can arm the Private Investigator to higher deliverable results. Part 4 covers setting up own business as a Private Investigator and marketing strategies besides organizational & analytical skills, ethics & obtaining evidences, with very useful Appendices containing forms and checklists.

Acknowledgement

I would like to thank Mr. Dinesh O Bareja, a well known stalwart in the field, to be a guiding light and inspiration to me. His persistent effort to safeguard the peripheries of the cyber domain has encouraged enthusiasts to explore various aspects of cyber crime and protection. Under this light, I found myself drawn to explore and conduct exhaustive research to compile a complete guide on private investigation.

The knowledge shared by Mr. Dinesh O Bareja on several aspects of cyber security was one of the encouraging factors that motivated me to undertake this venture and help the common people and enthusiasts learn about this aspect.

I would also like to extend my gratitude to everyone including my office staff that supported me during the compilation of this book. A special thanks to my wife, mother, and father, who kept the flame of inspiration in me ignited. As we progress with the new normal transforming our lifestyle across regions, cyberspace has also witnessed significant transformations, with the types of transactions on-boarding online platforms widening the array of loopholes for various crimes. In tandem with these, other crimes that are not linked with online platforms are finding various portals a route of their escape.

Author's Note:

This book is compiled for those who have want to spread their wings in investigations, but do not have the required basics in the field. The individuals whether one wants to work for some body or open their own Investigation Agency, can find the book very useful.

The book will lead you to a path to start your new venture in this domain either independently or with grooming and support from Cyber Crime Helpline LLP. If you like the book and the contents useful, wait for the advanced version!

Table of Content

Introduction

Many authors have written books on "Private Investigation" and have indicated that investigation reveals the truth. It's not a mere truth but at some point of time during the investigation process, the truth is not actually relevant. The only relevant thing at all times of all the stages of investigation process is "evidence". Evidence is considered as a direct proof describing the admissible facts of any incident or case. We all know that truth of any case could lead to admissible evidence. However, it is not necessary that the truth can always reveal itself and be admissible in court of law. A Private Investigator should be able to exploit any truth in favour of his case. His vision should be focussed on likely evidence for the benefit of the case.

However, "The Complete Private Investigator's Guide Book" is not just for detectives and working professionals, but it's also an invaluable resource for students and those seeking some opportunities to work with either the private detective agencies or in association with us in Cyber Crime Helpline LLP. The requirement to undertake background checks on employees or tenants, premarital, infidelity checks, etc would also otherwise be an evergreen necessity.

The book 'Complete Private Investigator's Guide Book' is designed for the following:

a) People who want to work as Private Investigator either full time or part time as a profession in this field, with complete guidance for their investigations.

b) One can work as Private Investigator irrespective whether they have an office or not.

c) Any one whether you are a school student, in college, housewife or working professionals, legal or technical professional, can find the book useful to setup own venture.

d) Those who want to work in free time and assist police or legal teams apart from victims when police complaint has been lodged.

One must have come across many books on the subject and must have traversed different claims to their investigative skills, but this is the book on the subject with a very different approach to investigation with conventional as well as digital means. Why is this book so different than already existing books? It would be evident once we ponder on the many prevalent detective agencies working in this field in a conventional manner without any involvement of the upcoming cyber methodologies to obtain the elusive evidences in the growing digital space. This book would cover on the latest methodology filled with technical acumen to gather evidential facts be it a murder, drug peddling, harassment, divorce, cheating/adultery infidelity, business/corporate investigations, etc. The topics included in the digital investigation, comprises practical methods to fact finding.

PART 1

Kit up your bags before you plunge into an adventurous journey of a professional Private Investigator

#One

Groom Yourself for Investigation

Now you find yourself interested in the novel profession of a Private Investigator! Whether you have a technical background or non technical, whether you are a working professional or intend working, this information and the course would suit all and you will be tempted to seek more and more technical knowhow on this unique course. This chapter has been designed to assist the Private Investigator to understand methods on equipping oneself with the required skills quickly.

1) Essential Skills?

Investigations are based on scientific analysis. Some important skills which would need to be exercised are observation, concentration, making instant notes and analysis of the evidential facts on the same day. Nobody is born with any skills and one has to develop this art for investigative purposes. All professionals develop their skills after undergoing training, education and acquiring knowledge. Similarly, skills mentioned above are considered essential for a Private Investigator. One has to just remind oneself that observation powers can also be enhanced with noting down certain dug out facts of any visual or scene as covered during the investigation.

Since curiosity leads us to higher observation and concentration skills, we would safely presume that anyone willing to work in the investigative domain can improve his concentration & observation skills. Observation & concentration are dependent upon one another and are generally based on results. One is expected to keep his/her eyes and ears always open and note down the implied analysis almost immediately.

If an Investigator loses his/her focus while investigating, he/she might lose the most powerful evidence in the case. During any surveillance, the investigator must always have an eye i.e. an uninterrupted focus on the target until the objective is achieved.

In fact, concentration & observation skills are the outcome of the confidence in their strategy in any type of investigation.

2) Skill Improvement

Research has shown that certain mental exercises add to the operating capacity of your brain, regardless of age, education, or experience.

Several techniques that deliver information from your short-term memory bank to your long-term memory bank are:

Repetition: Memorization of poems, numbers, words or scripture.

Consistent use of information: Complicated sequences of actions can be memorized by going through the sequences again and again.

Grouping: For instance, phone numbers are easier to remember when they are grouped between hyphens

Putting information to music: Most of us can still sing our ABCs

Mnemonics: Many techniques use either acronym or image to link the familiar with the unfamiliar---linking an image to the information you want to remember.

Besides exercises to improve overall function, several techniques can help improve concentration while one is on surveillance:

Breathing exercises. Breathe deeply & slowly through the nose, and then out through the mouth, pushing air from your lungs by sucking in your stomach.

Minimize distractions. Do nothing that may divert attention from the target. Minimize mobile distractions.

Comment aloud. Many investigators talk to themselves as they watch. Describing the house, office, and grounds into a tape recorder may help you later, when you write your report.

Snack. Most investigators eat to stay alert. But overeating may result in lethargic feeling.

If you use snacking, be aware that highly processed carbohydrates can make you sleepy, as can turkey and sugar products. Fruits, veggie sticks, cheese, nuts, or protein that can be eaten with your fingers and will ensure a steady supply of fuel to your brain. Highly processed food will provide a quick, momentary pickup, then drop your skills just as quickly. Following are the aspects one can bear in mind to enhance their skills in communication.

- ✓ Be positive with everyone; become genuinely interested in people
- ✓ Praise sincerely, but don't unnecessarily flatter.
- ✓ Be flexible and willing to consider another point of view
- ✓ Put your queries ----without criticizing or blaming any one
- ✓ Honour appropriate limits and respect the sentiments of others
- ✓ Just admit when you are wrong, but make appropriate corrections
- ✓ Do more listening than talking; encourage the other person to talk about himself
- ✓ Talk straight with subjects and suspects but with diplomacy.

3) Enhance your concentration

Practice to focus on a particular case with eyes open and then with eyes closed. Just see the difference in the brain's analytic powers. One can improve with exercise like TM, pondering over pros and cons of any eventuality and desire to get the result. One can play sudoku, scrabble, chess and crosswords-like games which leave some impact in mind on new ways to achieve the results. Similarly, one can download certain apps from their play store which helps one to sharpen their concentration & analytical skills. These apps claim that brain functions get triggered and may help one to sharpen one's concentrative powers.

4) Communicate with Patience

An investigator has to be a good communicator who not only expresses well but also lends his ears with great patience. The art of extracting information from others depends on patience and soft tactful leading queries to reveal vital information. Effective communication is an exchange of information between the applicant & investigator and subject & investigator.

Calm and composed communication brings optimum results in any type of investigation whether it was during the interview of any subject or interrogation of any suspect.

5) Listening Skills

Listening is the ability to accurately receive and interpret messages in the communication process. Effective listening is a skill that underpins all positive human relationships. Spend some time thinking about and developing your listening skills – they are the building blocks of success.

As per Forbes, the 10 steps to effective listening are enlisted as under:

- ✓ Face the speaker and maintain eye contact
- ✓ Be attentive but relaxed: a) Be present, b) Give attention, c) Apply or direct yourself, d) Pay attention, e) Remain ready to serve
- ✓ Keep an open mind
- ✓ Listen to the words and try to picture what the speaker is saying
- ✓ Don't interrupt or don't impose your solutions
- ✓ Wait for the speaker to pause to ask clarifying questions
- ✓ Ask question only to ensure understanding
- ✓ Try to feel what the speaker is feeling
- ✓ Give the speaker regular feedback by way of expression
- ✓ Pay attention to what is not said or hidden to reveal non-verbal cues.

One should record the conversation, listen to it, and then listen again. It's amazing how, after listening second or third time, changes your perspective and direction of investigation.

6) Perseverance and Patience

As per Swami Vivekanand, the valuable quotes on perseverance and patience, which are quite motivating, are as under:

- ✓ Are great things ever done smoothly? Time, patience, and indomitable will show.
- ✓ Every work has to pass through hundreds of difficulties before succeeding. Those that persevere will see the light, sooner or later.
- ✓ "Fortune favours the brave and energetic." Don't look back — forward, infinite energy, infinite enthusiasm, infinite daring, and infinite patience — then alone can great deeds be accomplished. We must set the whole world afire.
- ✓ Have patience and be faithful unto death. Do not fight among yourselves. Be perfectly pure in money dealings... We will do great things yet... So long as you have faith and honesty and devotion, everything will prosper.
- ✓ He who has infinite patience and infinite energy at his back, will alone succeed. Infinite patience, infinite purity, and infinite perseverance are the secret of success in a good cause.
- ✓ If you have infinite patience and perseverance, success is bound to come. No doubt in that.
- ✓ No need for looking behind. FORWARD! We want infinite energy, infinite zeal, infinite courage, and infinite patience, then only will great things be achieved.
- ✓ Nothing else is necessary but these — love, sincerity, and patience.
- ✓ Nothing shall be done in haste. Purity, patience, and perseverance are the three essentials to success and, above all, love.

- ✓ Take courage and work on. Patience and steady work — this is the only way. Go on; remember — patience and purity and courage and steady work. . . . So long as you are pure, and true to your principles, you will never fail.
- ✓ The fruit falls from the tree when it gets ripe. So wait for the time to come. Do not hurry. Moreover, no one has the right to make others miserable by his foolish acts. Wait, have patience, everything will come right in time.
- ✓ To succeed, you must have tremendous perseverance, tremendous will. Have that sort of energy, that sort of will, work hard, and you will reach the goal.

7) Quick Thinking and Discretion

For the successful investigator, the benefits of being able to think several steps ahead cannot be measured. Neither can discretion -- the ability to judge and make a decision regarding the relative importance of an event, statement, or item in relation to your investigation.

Proper use of discretion is probably the most important measure of an investigating officer.

It didn't take long to realize few things involved with human behaviour are black or white. The best cops operate in the grey areas of human existence. The grey area is where we as citizens need the police to operate with confidence and good judgment.

Discretion can only be used on minor crimes. Felony crimes are considered black and white. If you commit a felony, you should get locked up. Many times when a suspect is caught, booked and spends a night or two in jail, it may be the only time that person will spend behind bars.

An investigator must be able to think on his feet and make judgments quickly and sometimes within seconds. But the wrong judgment can jeopardise the case in hand.

Situations will result in the need to make difficult choices, think on your feet, and remain aware of your environment. Experience helps, as does thinking ahead. Some experts believe that the best decisions are made within seconds, but only if the person making the decision is knowledgeable about the situation.

Discretion is the quality of behaving or speaking in such a way as to avoid causing offence or revealing confidential information. It is the freedom to decide what should be done in a particular situation.

8) Ability to Recollect

Ability to recollect the immediate scenes or communication is based on the development of memory. There are three types of memory- **sensory, short term and long term**. They are all stored in different parts of the brain for different periods and using different methods.

Memory Enhancing Tips

As per Harvard Medical School, there are seven ways to keep your memory sharp at any age. They are:

- ✓ Keep learning
- ✓ Use all your senses
- ✓ Believe in yourself
- ✓ Economise your brain use
- ✓ Repeat what you may forget
- ✓ Memorise it at frequent interval.
- ✓ Make a mnemonic – acronym or relate it to some thing

9) Note-Taking

The best investigators record incidentals such as record the comings and goings of people and vehicles, not merely at the target residence or business, but in the surrounding area. This need not be included in your report unless proven relevant, but sometimes who or what is relevant won't be apparent until you have gathered more information, so record what you see and hear. These items are verifiable bits of information that create the perception of professionalism and boost the credibility of testimony.

When taking notes during interviews, write very little; jot only the main points, numbers, dates, etc. pay more attention to your subject than to your notebook, but as soon as possible, supplement your notes so that they make sense; otherwise, they may appear vague.

Writing Skills

Without some skill in writing, reports will appear unprofessional. Investigative report writing consists of the six basics taught in school; who, what, where, when, why, and how. Your investigation answers these questions. If you can't articulate who you investigated, what you found, where, when, and how you found it, and why it's important to your case, your investigative efforts are of little use to any client.

Today's private investigator can't throw a case together and rush to the next. Because information is his business, he must be capable of relaying that information in a clear manner. Professionally written communication, or the lack of it, can directly determine the size of fees that clients are willing to pay.

10) Keeping Secrets

If you have trouble keeping secrets or delight in telling bits of information about others to anyone who will listen, you must learn to tame that tongue. Not only can revealing sensitive or secret information put your case at risk, it can put your safety at risk as well.

If you spill the secrets of others to feel important, procure a confidante, gain notoriety, or obtain money, Private Investigator work is not for you. Secrets kept by investigators affect the lives of real people. If you have no understanding of this and no empathy for those whose secrets you hold, you're not investigator material.

#Two

Why a Private Investigator?

Why will one ever need a Private Investigator? Police departments don't have the manpower or the time to search indefinitely for any type of case except serious ones. Imagine parents who leave their spouses and children without paying support. When the trail becomes cold, they must usually direct their efforts toward other cases. At this point, the spouse may contact a Private Investigator in order to continue the search. Private Investigator's role here would be to supplement the actions of police and at the same time can team up with the applicant/victim for decisive strategies to achieve the objective. Now, consider the following aspects which will highlight the role and importance of a Private investigator:-

a) Manpower and priority is generally accorded to serious crimes or where media is involved, so if your client's case has lost its importance, hiring of a Private Investigator can supplement the police in the case and at the same time be approachable to the victim/applicant.

b) It is often seen that the victim keeps pondering whether such and such action has been taken by the police or not and so on, but discussion with a hired Private Investigator will give confidence and strength to seek legal support where police could have missed out.

c) Imagine there is a case of suicide and police is just waiting for the post-mortem report to close the case without establishing what bothered the deceased to take such a severe step. In this case, our trained Private Investigator can establish the facts which led to such a severe step.

d) The Private Investigator who is trained by us can reach the desired solution/evidence by digital means as well and also supplement the police where they would otherwise have gone later, subject to availability of technical staff.

e) If any serious theft or accident takes place, immediate hiring of a Private Investigator can not only assist the victim to give proper statements besides working independently to get to the suspect with the evidential facts.

f) The focus of a Private Investigator would be completely on victim/applicant's case where as same police personnel handle many cases simultaneously which may dilute the focus, thrust and attention to minor evidences.

1. Role at the Crime Scene

Private Investigators rarely deal with a crime scene, except under certain circumstances, and usually only after the police have abandoned it. The best action if you're the first to arrive at a crime scene is to touch nothing and call the police. However, should someone be injured and need help, or be in imminent danger of injury or death, you may be forced to enter the scene. In this case you need to know something about crime scene procedure and evidence handling.

Law enforcement officers follow a standard procedure for crime scene handling and processing. The most important rule in this procedure is protection of the scene. Only a few circumstances allow for anyone to enter a crime scene before it's been processed. The first, and most important, of these circumstances is threat of injury or death to someone inside.

Another circumstance in which police enter a crime scene before it's processed is if evidence could possibly be destroyed. For example, if drugs are known to be inside, there's a chance they will be flushed. In this case, police usually enter and prevent this destruction. However, most officers advise against the PI attempting to safeguard the scene, the private investigator should only preserve the scene until police arrive.

2. Preserving the Scene

Preserving a crime scene is the most important step in gathering evidence. Anyone who enters a scene brings something with him like fibres, hairs, or soil and takes something from the scene with him when he leaves. This exchange contaminates the scene. If you can do so, keep it from happening, but remember that you're not the police, and aren't in the enforcement business. Don't go so far as to use force or you could be looking at an assault charge yourself. Do what you can to help and let the police deal with any untoward incident.

3. Documenting the Scene

The purpose of a crime scene investigation is to discover what happened, how it happened, when it happened, determine the areas that show what happened, and who did it, or who committed the crime. What evidences are established and what evidences will need to be established should also be documented.

In furtherance of this goal, forms are used in the documentation of scenes. Everything can't be included on every form; therefore, forms vary from department to department. They're used not as substitutes for thinking, but as reminders of important steps to take in scene examination. Anything discovered that's not listed on the form can be added. Six categories of documentation are generally recognized as being applicable to any scene and are as follows:

- **Overview worksheet------**for recording all activity at the scene that relates to when, what, where, and how evidence is collected and preserved, and possible suspects
- **Scene worksheet------**for recording a narrative of the general, overall description of the crime scene and any impressions elicited from it
- **A diagram/sketch log----**for showing an overhead view of the entire scent, the location of physical evidence, as well as the distance of each piece of evidence from other objects in the scene

- **Photographic log**----for recording photographic views of the scene----specifically, overall or distant, medium, and close-up views of the scene and objects in it
- **Latent print lift log**---for documenting the collection, marking, and labelling of latent print lifts and the location in which they were found.
- **Evidence log**-----for documenting the collection, marking, and labelling of all evidence

A thorough documentation of any crime scene would include such observations as weather conditions, lighting, whether objects & furniture are out of place, disturbed, or destroyed; whether windows, curtains, and doors are open or closed; whether doors or windows are broken or display any type of damage or tool marks; whether emergency or medical teams have moved anything in order to work on a victim; and whether anything seems to be missing or might have been brought in and left by an offender.

#Three

Essentials: Your First Step

1. Digital Evidence and Extraction Tools

Before one takes a leap in this venture, one needs to know what digital evidences are important for his/her case. The list of self-explanatory evidences and essential tools, are enlisted here:

a) Photographs: These are essential, though the screenshots of what one finds on the social media, or research can be a vital evidence in your favour. The photograph's exif/metadata with hash is important to produce any digital evidence in the court of law.

b) Presence in Social Media: These are also good supplementary evidences to establish the subject could be an offender/accused.

c) Hash Tools: To obtain the hash (SHA1/SHA256) to establish the file integrity of the evidences required to submit for legal purposes. Tools and methods are explained during the training offered.

d) Exif tools: To get the meta data of the document/s obtained as evidence. This would indicate the date and time of creation of the file/document/audio/video. The tools are available freely.

e) Passwords of the subject: Though extraction of passwords of anybody is highly illegal, but when an investigator is trying to nab a fraudster or a hacker, one can consider this option to get more insight into his email or social media accounts. The extraction tool would assist to get the saved passwords of the suspect's accounts.

f) Wifi access tool:Its possible to extract wifi access of mobiles/laptops by such tools to establish earlier visits/association of the past, between the suspected couples.

g) Bluetooth pairing tool: This aspect can also throw significant light on sharing of media by means of Bluetooth pairing.

h) Events log: Event logs are evidential facts stored on a PC system and can be extracted by tools. Event logs contain time of switching on/off, system upgrades, applications installed, etc. Applications which get started also figure

i) Browser details: All browser passwords, caches, cookie information, history can be extracted by tools. For more about tools, email us your request on the given email id at the last page of the book.

2. Checklist/Preparation

Outfit of Investigator for physical shadowing a subject. It is recommended to have at least two outfits in their kits to avoid any suspicion.

a) Specs/goggles can further assist the investigator to modify their appearance beyond recognition.

b) Forms, Questionnaire and Tasking Sheet would be prove beneficial to obtain complete information provided by the applicant who is hiring you for any case, as covered during the training.

c) USB Drive and Laptop would help the investigator to carry necessary tools to dig the suspect out in the digital arena.

d) Camera/Mobile which can take photographs would help gather photographs as much as possible.

e) Log book to record details of events with time.

3. Vehicle Readiness

Suitability of vehicle for shadowing may depend on whether the subject you are following is having which vehicle? In all respects a four-wheeler or hired cab/car could prove beneficial. It also depends on the destination/likely destination of the subject to help one decide of vehicle or directly reaching the target destination.

4. Day and Time for Shadowing

Day and time to shadow can be dependent on whether the subject's movement to office or any other destination, whether it is rainy season or where night following is concerned. The devices to capture evidences and complete shadowing/tracking preparations will be based on where to expect the subject and what time of the day, etc.

5. Avoid these Mistakes

There are few things that the Private Investigator will need to cater. These points are best to be avoided as it can put you to trouble. The aspects to avoid are enlisted below:-

- ✓ Do not share all your information, strategy or plan of action to the applicant as they might reveal it to their near and dear ones and jeopardise your efforts.
- ✓ Do not visit the applicant in your disguised outfit.
- ✓ Better avoid disclosing your movement details with your applicants.
- ✓ Do not be shabbily dressed while visiting your applicant. Don't get overdressed too. Good/polished footwear, combed hair, no perfume, etc will help.
- ✓ Do not discuss over the phone without first meeting the client face to face
- ✓ Do not offer your services without any indication of output/result.

PART 2

The Detective way to Investigations

#Four

Woking Methodology of an Investigator

1) Initial Steps

A Private Investigator must take certain steps at the outset. Though the steps varies with the type of case/s, the strategy may need to be defined well. These steps involve paperwork and analysis, but they are absolutely necessary for obtaining the best possible outcome. In fact, a preliminary analysis, or subject profile, will aid in all types of investigations. Most of the cases involve missing / absconding persons or cheating cases.

Create a Profile and Determine Motivation

Creating a profile of the absconder will help one a great deal in the long run. The investigator will need to pen down his/her thought process and aspects that will need to be checked before it fades away from the mind.

- ✓ The necessary information of the subject in many case/s will be as under:
- ✓ Personal Information: Complete Name with aliases, if any, physical attributes like hair/eye colour, specks (distant/near vision), habits/hobbies, and other details given by the applicant.
- ✓ Associations: Friend list with emphasis of best friends (in both sexes).
- ✓ His/her job, role and responsibilities with present employer and previous employers (with durations) besides his educational qualifications and skill/expertise aspects
- ✓ His/her vehicle details, with insurance expiry information
- ✓ His/her computer knowledge and skills. Whether the subject had laptop/PC, etc

- ✓ Details of his/her outstation visits in the last one year.
- ✓ The debit/credit cards owned by him and how many bank accounts did he have? Did he carry the cards and/or valuables?
- ✓ The details of his/her medical state of last one year.

2) Crime Scene and Evidence Handling

Evidence is the backbone of all investigations. However, its efficacy lies in the manner in which it's handled, collected, stored and presented. Mistakes committed by untrained investigators may include:

- ✓ Time stamping of evidence
- ✓ Recognizing the evidence as vital
- ✓ Labelling and storing the evidence and whether it will be used as exhibit in the court of law or not.
- ✓ Photo evidence and log book maintained by the investigator.
- ✓ Whether or not external experts like fingerprinting experts or handwriting experts is required or not.
- ✓ Involvement of forensic science experts to establish firearm/weapon injury marks can also be ascertained besides Lie detectors and audio spectroscopy experts.

3) Preserving the Chain of Custody

It is important to pay attention to the preservation of any evidence which may be required to be produced in court. Following aspects will need to be adhered to with utmost sincerity:

- ✓ Carry couple of poly pouches/envelopes, labels to stick on these pouches.
- ✓ Allocate the evidence number and record it in the log book regarding place and time of collection. In some evidences, photographs may be beneficial.

- ✓ Hashing of digital evidences and preserving in a folder on ausb drive. SHA256 hash is recommended so as to avoid hash collisions.
- ✓ Record the handling of evidence against the handler's name in the custody records. For example 'A' collected the evidence namely a pen drive from a crime scene. The date, time of collection with location/from person will need to be recorded and when this pen drive is given to the storekeeper, it should have been labelled and packed and again recorded as to the time handed over to the storekeeper. The recording of custody details should continue till it is handed over to the authorised government personnel for further course of action.

Five

Introduction to Handwriting and Fingerprinting

1) Handwriting Examination

In certain case/s there may be requirement to verify signature or the handwriting of a subject. There are many authorised labs which will assist you in providing professional services in your city. Handwriting of a person is his writing which may be alphabet, words, signature, initials, digits or figures written in some script or non-script form. It is usually written by hand but.The question here is why will a victim ever need the services of a handwriting examination? Some scenarios are enlisted below:

- ✓ To seek permission of court for verification of a person subject to his/her case.
- ✓ When the authenticity of the writer or author of the handwriting or signature is in doubt handwriting/Signature verification is done

Points to remember while submitting the handwriting to the authorities like police/court or any authorised agency:

- ✓ Mark the handwritings with signature as doubtful.
- ✓ Give as much writings as possible. A page could suffice. The quality should be good. Scanned documents should be clear. Don't crop or edit the images in .jpg or .jpeg formats.
- ✓ Submission of handwriting and signature in the court should be handled by the applicant's lawyer.

Handwriting analysis is also considered at times to assess the character of the candidate during the selection process in many organisation. The most common attributes in general are: dedication & devotion, loyalty, ambition, sexual orientation,

2) Fingerprinting

The ridge lines on the palms of the hands and the fingers leave impressions on the surface either visible or invisible, are collected during this process.

Hand and fingerprints are required to prove the authenticity of a person. Since no two people have same fingerprints, this accurately establishes identification. Care should be taken not to smudge the fingerprints, others should not handle and it should be stored in normal humid conditions i.e neither in high nor in low humid conditions.

The fingerprinting involves following steps:

a) Lifting/collection of fingerprints

b) Packaging and safety

c) Analysis by an authorised professional

Materials required for collection of fingerprints ink, fingerprint lifting tapes, powders, evidence pouches/envelopes can be easily set up if required at a later stage. Keep the contact details of authorised fingerprinting professionals handy.

#Six

Conventional Investigations

The conventional investigations are limited to simple interrogations, gathering information from the third parties by known accomplices or by greasing the palms of the evidence providers. The types of conventional investigations can be broadly categorised in the following types:

1) Cheating Cases

The erstwhile conventional detective would otherwise seek information of the suspected person, mutual associations be it friends, relatives or service providers to question and form an opinion. The conventional detective also undertakes shadowing of the suspect to gather photographic evidences. Audio/video bugging devices are also used by the conventional detectives. Cheating cases are a bit difficult to prove in the court of law. The Appendix at the end of the chapter can provide you the generalised but indicative assessment of a cheating spouse.

2) Divorce, Infidelity and Child Custody Investigations

The investigation of divorce, infidelity and child custody investigations are based on the inputs given by the applicant. It also involves shadowing, bugging with audio and video bugging devices. It will be covered in detail in Part 3 in which the cyber detective can gather substantial evidences by digital means.

Emotions arising of frustrations in job/s, relationship and ego are the causes of domestic disharmony. One partner or the other who are not able to resolve their differences mutually land themselves in volatile situation.

3) Investigating Infidelity

If a partner/spouse is suspected of infidelity, there has to be reasons to suspect. While the person/applicant may be analysing unexplained behaviour patterns, the suspicion can be, to some extent be ascertained on the basis of our checklist at appendix. The checklist is quite elaborative and it helps the investigator to prepare his/her tasking sheet based on which one can acquire adequate inputs to plan a strategy.

4) Divorce and Infidelity Investigations

Divorce cases are filed in family courts and are in some cases a FIR/complaint is made by one of the partner against the other in the police station. The lawyer of the opponent side may like to contract out investigative needs. Here comes to put a ploy your person as having the required skills to get the factual details in hand.

A private investigator will often be asked to provide proof that a spouse is cheating.

Many times, the client or attorney needs to prove that the target has been guilty of infidelity, is unfit to care for children, or is in possession of hidden assets and so on. Remember that not every case ends in divorce; sometimes people reconcile too. If your client expresses the desire to work through his/her marriage, avoid being a counsellor. If your assistance is sought to negotiate, the opponent party will anyway take you as hostile.

Perform a background check. Do a practice-run by the subject's home, workplace, and any areas he frequents (such as a bar, golf course, country club, and possible girlfriend's home and work, particular joints they visit and so on).

5) Premarital & Infidelity Investigations

It's no longer only the wealthy who are concerned with the background of future mates. Premarital investigations have become highly popular in recent years. Many an unscrupulous man or woman has latched onto someone with a steady income, good credit, and a need for short time companionship.

It's easy for someone to hide her true history and identity today. Our mobile society, where even neighbours are strangers, lends the con artist anonymity. Anonymity can lead to ease of deception. If the client has any doubt, the person she suspects should be checked out.

6) Collecting photographic evidences

The practice of baiting a spouse or partner who is suspected of being a serial philanderer is a controversial type of investigation. The service provides pictures of trained investigators, and the client chooses one he believes to be the target's "type." The chosen bait wears a hidden camera and goes to an area the target is known to frequent. He may not approach the target, but may be receptive to her approaches.

7) Child Custody

Child custody is most often associated with divorce, but divorce is not the only circumstance that brings up the need for custody investigations. Today, for many reasons, grandparents and other family members regularly petition the courts for custody of minor children. Even friends of the family have been known to get involved and go to an investigator. As with divorce, these cases can be messy. Motives are not always pure, and emotions can be volatile on all sides.

8) Insurance Frauds

In the event of insurance frauds, the conventional detective collects the information of the fraudster's office address, residential address, his contact details, his company details and addresses, bank details of beneficiary and his other associates/victims, if any. The conventional detective then chalks out his strategy to trace the accused and gather evidence by collecting information.

Insurance Overview

Insurance is a contact between the insured, who agrees to pay for services, and the insurer, who agrees to provide monetary reimbursement for certain losses that may be incurred by the insured. There are two very wide categories of insurance: government insurance and private insurance, each divided into industries. Government insurance can be divided into compulsory and voluntary. While private insurance is usually divided into four sectors: casualty, fire, life, and water.

The sites pertaining to India are as under:

The NSDL website: https://nir.ndml.in/

National Insurance Fraud Investigators

(https://www.india.gov.in/official-website-serious-fraud-investigation-office)

The National Insurance Fraud Investigators office was organized to serve a broad membership like insurance companies, law enforcement and bond enforcement officers, information services, forensic examiners, skip tracers, investigators, security specialists, and attorneys in India. Membership includes access to networking opportunities, education and training, and a newsletter filled with up-to-date information on fraud investigations.

Government Compulsory Insurance can be:

- Unemployment benefits in some countries
- Social Security benefits
- Workers' compensation in many states
- Travel insurance by air or rail

Government Voluntary Insurance examples:

- Savings and loans and bank depositor insurance
- Crop/Yield insurance
- Military personnel insurance
- Natural Calamity insurance
- Accident insurance

Private insurance is voluntary, except for the compulsory (basic collision) automobile insurance required on all drivers in most states. There are many types of private insurance, but some of the basic types are listed below.

Basic Types of Private Insurance

- Life
- Home
- Rental
- Automobile/flight/accidents
- Health and medical
- Special insurance

It's important to be familiar with appropriate terms in order to work in the insurance industry. Knowing something of the most used terms will also help you when interviewing for a position investigating insurance fraud.

9) Personal Injury Investigations

Personal injury cases take a toll on both businesses and individuals. Legitimate injuries caused by the negligence of businesses are needless tragedies, and businesses should recompense the injured adequately. Sometimes, however, unscrupulous persons construct fake accidents and sue businesses, hoping for settlements out of court. If they can manage this, there's usually no great spotlight on the details of the accident and injury. Furthermore, many companies find if less time consuming and much expensive to pay someone who's threatening a lawsuit than to go to court.

10) Accident Investigations

With regards to the accident investigations, the conventional detectives gather information from the volunteered witnesses, nearby shops, vehicle insurance companies, driving licenses of both the parties and their id proofs to find legal ways to handle/advise the lawyer during the court trial.

11) Murder/Suicide Cases

These types of investigations are generally covered by conventional detectives by gathering information provided by the applicant, friend or relatives of the deceased person and by interrogating known enemies of the deceased. Information pertaining to involvement of a woman/girl, loan, serious illness or embarrassing events which would have surfaced otherwise may also lead the deceased to take such a serious step or get trapped in any murderous conspiracy. These cases too are handled by the cyber detectives as covered in Part 3.

12) Finding Whereabouts of Fraudster

This is one of the most sought after requirement which is linked to many types of investigations. The conventional detectives would try to gather information by means of social engineering (extracting information from third parties without revealing their motive). The people whom the conventional detective could gather information from may vary from the last known person who saw the subject leaving a particular place, friends, associates and relatives of the subject, his previous office or residential addresses, his regular/routine visits to any club or gym, etc. Address finding can be simplified by digital means as covered in Part 3 later.

13) Spouse/Child's Activity

With the rise in social media addictions and exposure to internet resources of various kinds by their children's unethical/wrongful or unsocial indulgence is a cause of concernfor many parents/spouse. Since the child of minor age also has full access to any mobile/laptop, his immaturity or emotions is most likely to lead him/her astray on a wrong/illegal/unethical path. This fear amongst parents is one of the main cause to know or monitor the child's activity. Similarly, the hectic and busy schedule of husband or wife or both also raises suspicion whether or not the spouse is having a platonic or extra marital relationship at the work place or out of home adventures. In such cases, the conventional detective primarily works on shadowing the subject to gather photographic evidences.

14) Missing/Absconding Cases

The methodology of a conventional detective for the missing or absconding fraudster is similar to cases where address finding or cheating/infidelity cases are concerned. This is adequately covered in a dedicated chapter for missing persons besides locating the subject digitally in Part 3.

15) Background checks

A conventional detective undertakes background checks by enquiring from friends, neighbours, educational institutes, clubs, his/her friend circle or his known enemies if any. This could help resolve many types of case/s including financial investigations too wherein the conventional detective would gather information from his bank and online searches. This type of cases is better investigated as per digital methodology as covered in the later chapters.

16) DNA and Blood group Investigations

DNA Testing:

Establishing links between leads can be very difficult. However, today with advanced laboratory and forensics analysis, we can use DNA evidence to fill in the gaps in your investigation. DNA has found the missing link in many of our cases. We can assist in the later evaluation of crime scene evidence.

- Who is sending threatening or harassing letter?
- Who is the father of the child?
- Is someone intimate with my spouse?
- Whose cigarette butts are these at the scene?

Test artefacts and objects for DNA investigations, testing, and analysis:

- Cigarette Butts
- Discarded Gum
- Bottle Top
- Toothbrush
- Hair follicle and Hair
- Bodily Fluids
- Skin Oil Residue
- Skin Residue
- Saliva
- Blood Residue

Anything which has been touched can be tested and analysed in the forensics labs.

Blood-group Donor & Receptors:

There are 4 main blood groups (types of blood) – A, B, AB and O. Your blood group is determined by the genes you inherit from your parents. Each group can be either RhD positive or RhD negative, which means in total there are 8 blood groups.

Blood group donors and receptors are as under:

A+ve: Can donate to A+ve&AB+ve and receive from A+ve, O+ve, A-ve, O-ve

O+ve:Can donate to A+ve,B+ve. O+ve,AB+ve and receive O+ve, O-ve

B+ve: Can donate to B+ve&AB+ve and receive from B+ve, B-ve, O-ve, O+ve

AB+ve:Can donate to AB+ve and receive from all blood groups

A-ve: Can donate to A+ve, A-ve, AB+ve& AB-ve and receive from A-ve, O-ve

O-ve: Can donate to everyone and receive from O-ve

B-ve: Can donate to B+ve,B-ve,AB+ve& AB-ve and receive from B-ve, O-ve

AB-ve: Can donate to AB+ve& AB-ve and receive from A-ve, O-ve, AB-ve, B-ve

Offspring probability:

Parents Blood Types: A, A: Possible Child: A,ONot Possible: B, AB

Parents Blood Types: A, B: Possible Child: A, O, B, ABNot Possible: Nil

Parents Blood Types: A, AB: Possible Child: A, B, AB Not Possible: O

Parents Blood Types: A, O: Possible Child:A, O Not Possible: B, AB

Parents Blood Types: B, B: Possible Child: B, O Not Possible: A, AB

Parents Blood Types: B, AB:Possible Child: A, B, AB Not Possible: O

Parents Blood Types: B, O: Possible Child: B, ONot Possible: A, AB

Parents Blood Types: AB, AB: Possible Child: A, B, AB Not Possible: O

Parents Blood Types: AB, O: Possible Child: A, BNot Possible: AB, O

Parents Blood Types: O, O: Possible Child: O Not Possible: A, B, AB

Similarly for Rh factor –ve blood groups. Parents with different Rh factors may have complications. Blood group U (In Driving Licence) means that the blood group information is not available.

17) Drug Investigations

Some basic information about the most prevalent so called rape drugs and their affects are enumerated in the succeeding paragraphs.

What is Ecstasy (MDMA)

MDMA (3-4 methylenedioxymethamphetamine) is a synthetic, psychoactive drug with a chemical structure similar to the stimulant methamphetamine and the hallucinogen mescaline. MDMA is an illegal drug that acts as both a stimulant and psychedelic, producing an energizing effect, as well as distortions in time and perception and enhanced enjoyment from tactile experiences. It is known commonly as Ecstasy and Molly.

This illicit drug exerts its primary effects in the brain on neurons that use the chemicals serotonin, dopamine and norepinephrine to communicate with other neurons. Serotonin is most likely responsible for the feelings of empathy, elevated mood, and emotional closeness experienced with this drug. Overall, these neurotransmitter systems play an important role in regulating:

- ✓ mood
- ✓ energy/activity and the reward system
- ✓ appetite
- ✓ aggression
- ✓ sexual activity
- ✓ sleep
- ✓ sensitivity to pain
- ✓ heart rate, blood pressure

Gamma-hydroxybutyrate (GHB)

Gamma-hydroxybutyrate (GHB) is a central nervous system depressant. GHB is a clear, odourless liquid that looks like water and so can be added to a beverage without the person knowing it. It may also be used in the form of a white powder. GHB is also known as liquid ecstasy, soap, Easy Lay, and Georgia Home Boy.

Until 1992, GHB was sold in health food stores in products to build muscle tissue and to reduce body fat. Today, it can be obtained over the Internet and often is available at all-night dances, raves, and nightclubs.

At low doses, the drug relaxes the person. The person feels intoxicated, has more energy, feels happy, and is talkative. Other effects include:

Feeling affectionate and playful.

Mild loss of inhibition.

Increased sensuality.

Enhanced sexual feelings.

GHB can cause unwanted side effects, such as headache, drowsiness, dizziness, and vomiting. It can lead to difficulty breathing, being conscious but unable to move, and loss of consciousness—especially when it is combined with alcohol or other drugs. GHB has been involved in overdoses, date rapes, and death.

This drug does not stay in a person's system very long and is not easily detected with drug screening tests (toxicology tests).

Rohypnol

Rohypnol, a trade name for flunitrazepam, is a central nervous system depressant. It is similar to diazepam (such as Valium) but about 10 times more potent. It is commonly called rophies, roofies, roach, or rope. It is a tasteless, odourless tablet that can be crushed and dissolved in liquid. It has been used in date rapes, because it can be slipped into a person's drink without it being detected. One small tablet can produce effects for 8 to 12 hours.

Rohypnol is sometimes used to enhance the high of heroin or to ease the negative effects of a crack or cocaine binge. When Rohypnol is mixed with alcohol, its effects cause a person to not resist sexual assault. It can produce a form of amnesia so that the person may not remember what happened while under the influence of the drug. Rohypnol may lead to death when mixed with alcohol or other depressant drugs.

Ketamine

Ketamine is an anesthetic that is used primarily by veterinarians and by doctors who perform surgery on young children. It is also known as Special K, Super K, vitamin K, or simply as K. It is a liquid that can be snorted or injected. Ketamine use has become common in nightclubs, at all-night dances, and at raves. It has been used as a date rape drug.

At low doses, ketamine causes a tingling sensation, a loss of time perception often described as "eternity," and a perceived ability to determine causal connections between things.

At high doses, it distorts the person's perception of his or her body and the surroundings. The person may fall into a dreamlike state (catatonia) in which he or she has a flat facial appearance, an open mouth, a fixed stare with wide pupils, and a rigid posture. The person will withdraw socially, have autistic behaviour, and say bizarre things. This catatonic state is commonly called a K-hole.

At high doses, ketamine can cause delirium, amnesia, impaired motor function, high blood pressure, depression, paranoia, and severe breathing problems. Overdoses pose a serious life-threatening situation and need to be treated in a hospital and most often in an intensive care unit.

What is a date rape drug?

Date rape drugs are used to make a person more vulnerable to sexual assault and easier to attack. Sometimes, one or more drugs are used to distract a person so they become unaware of what's going on and unable to protect themselves. These drugs are often secretly slipped into someone's drink.

The most well-known date rape drugs include the following:

Rohypnol (flunitrazepam) is prescribed to people with sleep and anxiety disorders in other countries, but it's not approved for medical use in the United States. It's commonly called roofies or R-2.

GHB, or gamma hydroxybutyric acid, is sometimes prescribed to treat narcolepsy. It's also called cherry meth, liquid E, or scoop.

Ketamine is used during surgical procedures. It may be called vitamin K, cat valium, Kit Kat, or special K.

Less commonly used date rape drugs include:

ecstasy, also called Molly, X, and E

LSD, commonly called acid

clonazepam (Klonopin)

alprazolam (Xanax)

Symptoms of date rape drugs

When a date rape drug begins to cause symptoms and how long they last depends on how much you are given and whether it's mixed with alcohol or other drugs. Alcohol can make the effects even stronger. Symptoms of date rape drugs generally include dizziness, confusion, and loss of memory.

Rohypnol

The effects are typically felt within 30 minutes and include:

- slurred speech
- feeling very drunk, even if you've only had one drink
- dizziness
- unconsciousness
- loss of muscle control
- nausea
- confusion
- memory loss
- blackouts
- lowered blood pressure

GHB

Theeffects of GHB start in about 15 minutes. A tiny amount of GHB can have a major effect. GHB can cause these symptoms:

- drowsiness and dizziness
- vision problems
- feelings of relaxation
- increased sensuality
- seizures
- memory loss
- sweating
- slow heart rate
- nausea and vomiting

- blackouts
- loss of consciousness
- Ketamine

Ketamine begins to take effect very quickly, sometimes just a minute after ingestion. It can lead to:

- distorted perceptions of sight and sound
- out-of-body or dream-like experiences
- problems breathing
- loss of coordination
- convulsions
- numbness
- violent behavior
- high blood pressure

Date rape drugs affect on your body

Date rape drugs are powerful. Rohypnol is a central nervous system depressant or tranquilizer. GHB was formerly used as an anesthetic, and ketamine is a painkiller and anesthetic. In general, they cause drowsiness, slow your heart rate, and have a sedative effect on the body.

The resulting loss of inhibition, impaired judgement, and memory loss are reasons why these drugs are used in rape. They are sometimes called "paralyzing" since the person often loses muscle control and is unable to move or call for help.

Recognizing a date rape drug

Most date rape drugs are colorless, odorless, and tasteless. It may be impossible to tell if your drink has one in it. Ketamine comes in liquid, powder, or capsule form. GHB is made as both a white powder and a colorless, odorless liquid. GHB sometimes tastes a bit salty.

Rohypnol comes as a white, dime-sized pill that dissolves quickly in liquids. The manufacturer has changed the formulation so that when dissolved in liquid, it turns the liquid blue. This might help someone spot whether their drink has been tampered with. Generic versions of the pill don't have this feature.

Don't be surprised that in some part of the world there are men who fear sexual assault!!. The men are generally given Viagra or its equivalent drugs easily obtained over the counter.

In the Indian context, the known drug as desi variant of Viagra is called Penegra. This pills are considered cheap and freely available. Many women also prefer taking such pills/tablets to enhance blood flow to their genitals resulting in high libido. It affects within 30 minutes after taking the medication and may last for 4-6 hours. Can be fatal for patients on medication with nitrates or for cardio-vascular patients.Temporary loss of colour vision, nausea and headache.

The illegal use of drug and drug abuse cases can be complaint on the NCB by email on narcoticsbureau@nic.in and adops-ncb@nic.in

18) Corruption Investigations

The CBI is a central investigation agency with its headquarters in New Delhi, which investigates crimes that are either referred to it by the other states or that violate the Prevention of Corruption Act 1988 (POCA) in India. The DRI investigates violations of the Customs Act 1962 and is also an intelligence agency. Similarly, other countries will have similar procedures.

Detection mechanisms: Auditing and Reporting

- Audits: traditional and blockchain - important methods used to detect corruption in both public and private sector organizations is the auditing process

- Self-reporting
- Citizen reporting
- Journalism and media reporting
- Whistle-blowing
- Whistle-blowing versus leaking

Reporting Corruption in India

In India, one can file corruption complaints with at least three government-established bodies. Two of these three—the Central Vigilance Commission and the Central Bureau of Investigation—work in tandem. First, there is the Central Vigilance Commission (CVC). Established in 1964, this is a central level body.

You can contact your nearest Anti-Corruption official in person or through telephone or even email. More information can be obtained even on phone through the Toll Free numbers: 1800 233 44444 or 1064. The complaint can be filed with the Deputy Superintendent of Police or Inspector of Police.

Complaints can also be lodged by addressing the written communication/letter directly to the Commission or on Commission's portal www.portal.cvc.gov.inor through the Commission's website www.cvc.gov.in under the link "Lodge Complaint" on home page (http://portal.cvc.gov.in/cvproject/citizenRegister).

Website: http://cvc.gov.in

You can lodge your complaints at CBI official website. You can contact CBI office to fight corruption via telephone, CBI phone number – 011-24361273/2755/2357 or send mail on CBI mail ID – sphq@cbi.gov.in or report by email ids allocated to states under contact us page. Website: https://cbi.gov.in

In case of conviction, imprisonment is awarded from 6 months to 10 years. Anyone with assets disproportionate to his income commits 'criminal misconduct'

Conduct Rules for Government Employees

- Intimation about all moveable/immoveable property required at the time of joining civil service
- No acquisition of immoveable property without previous knowledge of govt.
- Every transaction exceeding Rs. 15000 in India (approximately $200 as per current exchange rate at the time of writing this book) to be informed of within a month
- Annual return in respect of immoveable property
- Can accept gifts from friends and relatives on special occasions, within Rs. 5000 ($67)
- No speculation in stocks/shares

19. Human Trafficking Investigations

A report on sex trafficking in India undertaken in 2014 was named 'Dasra report'as per which approximately 16 million women are victims of sex trafficking in India every year, while 40 per cent of them are adolescents and children. And more than 70 per cent of victims are illiterate and 50 per cent of them have a family income of less than $1 per day. Human Trafficking is considered as a serious crime and can be investigated and reported by the private investigator.

Human Trafficking

The United Nations organization defines **human trafficking** asthe recruitment, transportation, transfer, harboring, or receipt of persons by improper means (such as force, abduction, fraud, or coercion) for an improper purpose including forced labor or sexual exploitation. It takes on many forms today.

Trafficking in Human Beings or Persons is prohibited under the Constitution of India under Article 23 (1) The Immoral Traffic (Prevention) Act, 1956 (ITPA) is the premier legislation for prevention of trafficking for commercial sexual exploitation

Constitutional &Legislative Provisions Related to Trafficking in India

- ✓ Trafficking in Human Beings or Persons is prohibited under the Constitution of India under Article 23 (1)
- ✓ The Immoral Traffic (Prevention) Act, 1956 (ITPA) is the premier legislation for prevention of trafficking for commercial sexual exploitation.
- ✓ Criminal Law (amendment) Act 2013 has come into force wherein Section 370 of the Indian Penal Code has been substituted with Section 370 and 370A IPC which provide for comprehensive measures to counter the menace of human trafficking including trafficking of children for exploitation in any form including physical exploitation or any form of sexual exploitation, slavery, servitude, or the forced removal of organs.
- ✓ Protection of Children from Sexual offences (POCSO) Act, 2012, which has come into effect from 14th November, 2012 is a special law to protect children from sexual abuse and exploitation. It provides precise definitions for different forms of sexual abuse, including penetrative and non-penetrative sexual assault, sexual harassment.
- ✓ There are other specific legislations enacted relating to trafficking in women and children Prohibition of Child Marriage Act, 2006, Bonded Labour System (Abolition) Act, 1976, Child Labour (Prohibition and Regulation) Act, 1986, Transplantation of Human Organs Act, 1994, apart from specific Sections in the IPC,

e.g. Sections 372 and 373 dealing with selling and buying of girls for the purpose of prostitution.

- ✓ State Governments have also enacted specific legislations to deal with the issue. (e.g. The Punjab Prevention of Human Smuggling Act, 2012)

To report in India, call Shakti Vahini on +91-11-42244224, +91-9582909025 or the national helpline Childline on 1098. For different countries, refer to web search on government site links.

Seven

Disguising Oneself While Investigating

Conventional detectives will need to disguise himself/herself to evade the likely suspicion of the bystander on their movements whilst following the suspect/subject. The preparations and the major items generally catered for are enumerated in the succeeding paragraphs.

1) **Wigs.** There are many types of wigs available in the market for men and ladies which can camouflage your appearance if one has to look different.

2) **Profile Creation.** Any private investigator should have multiple profiles in the digital platform. If one's name is Sunil Srivastava, he can create profile as S. Srivastava or just Sunil or SS, etc so that he can present his name separately for different type of profile creation. Creation of profile means his separate emails for his separate names, his LinkedIn profiles, his advertisement in Just Dial or similar advertising/resourcing agencies, etc and that too with different types of job roles or advertisement. The job roles could be computer technician, consultant, distributor/reseller of any product, masseur, marketing executive of any bank, physiotherapist, yoga trainer, tuition teacher of particular grade or subject, etc. And the true caller account should accordingly be created to cater for this aspect.

3) **Mobile Numbers.** The private investigator is also expected to have around 2-4 mobile numbers for such profiles. One is expected to have couple of mobiles too for different types of profiles.

4) **Emails.** Besides his one email of private investigator, he is expected to have different emails for his handsets as per profiles. He should have couple of social media accounts like FB, Instagram, etc for boy and for girls too to enter into the digital lives of his subject for gaining confidence and gathering information.

5) **Dresses.** Every person has a unique way of dressing up, but the private investigator should preferably have couple of different types of dresses whilst shadowing the suspect/subject. If one uses spectacles, then have couple of different colour/shades of specs and if one doesn't use any spectacle, then may be at least one plain glass coloured spectacle may help the investigator to disguise him/herself.

Eight

Search and Surveillance

The laws governing this are the Indian Telegraph Act, 1885, which deals with interception of calls, and the Information Technology (IT) Act, 2000, which deals with interception of data. Under both laws, only the government, under certain circumstances, is permitted to conduct surveillance, and not private actors. Moreover, hacking is expressly prohibited under the IT Act. Section 43 and Section 66 of the IT Act cover the civil and criminal offences of data theft and hacking respectively. Section 66B covers punishment for dishonestly receiving stolen computer resource or communication. The punishment includes imprisonment for a term which may extend to three years.Inspite of the stringent laws, the requirement of a private investigator can be felt in every household as there is always some investigation which the police is overlooking or not able to get adequate proofs for any suspect in view of time constraint to shadow the subject and collect the evidence. Hiring of private investigator solves this aspect and the evidence collected by him/her can be produced in the court of law legally. Investigators spend most of their time doing some type of surveillance or other as its strategy is based on the success of your business. Some devices and methodologies are explained in the succeeding paragraphs.

1) Sting Operation

A sting operation is a disguised operation to catch a person while committing a crime. Insting operations, recording of video/audio toobtain evidence in order to expose the criminal activity is used.Sting operations are undertaken by the hired Private Investigators too to expose the subject.

2) Audio/Video Recording Laws

Investigation should take place with two-sided consent, i.e with the consent of both parties. All such evidence could be used to produce the recording in court and hence adequate reasons should be there before it can be brought in front of the court. It is generally seen that the client leaks the details about audio recording to the other party or known/unknown people who could pass the information to the other party.

3) Conventional Search Techniques

With all the sophisticated tools available, don't forget that, depending on the type of skip, it could take less time to use old-fashioned techniques. After having narrowed your search to a specific area, one can work on the following methods:-

a) Sending a letter or parcel to the last known address by a private delivery boy could reveal if the subject resides there or has moved to a different known area.

b) Searching in the paid lookup sites for his social media profiles could reveal his new job and or details.

c) The known friends who were close to the subject might reveal his actual location/address inadvertently provided if he is interrogated in an intelligent manner.

d) Proxy calling on his mobile numbers posing as insurance agents or vehicle insurance agents or his mobile number is being used from two locations, etc can also reveal certain facts about his location/address.

4) What is Stalking?

Stalking is defined as harassing or threatening behaviour that is engaged in repeatedly. Such harassment can be either physical stalking or cyber stalking. Here we have covered physical and cyber stalking and its repercussions. Following paragraphs under this topic is sourced from the hunter.cuny.edu and moderated to the present day situations.

Physical Stalking is committed when a person intentionally and for no legitimate purpose, engages in a course of conduct directed at a specific person, and knows or reasonably should know that such conduct is likely to cause fear of material harm to the physical, mental, or emotional health, safety or property of such person, a member of such person's immediate family or a third party with whom he or she is acquainted. This could include creating reasonable fear that such person's employment, business or career is being threatened. This is typically accomplished by following someone or appearing at their home, school or place of business, making harassing phone calls, leaving messages or objects, or vandalizing the person's property.

Cyber Stalking is similar behaviour through the use of the internet or other electronic means to accomplish the similar end. The fact that cyber stalking doesn't involve physical contact doesn't mean that it is less dangerous than physical stalking. An experienced Internet user can easily find the victim's personal information such as phone number, address or place of business to locate their whereabouts. This can then lead to more physical behaviour. Stalking is defined as a crime in many countries.

There are several signs that are good indicators of stalking behaviour:

- ✓ Persistent phone calls and/or text messages despite being told not to contact the victim in any form.
- ✓ Waiting at or outside the victim's workplace, residence or school.
- ✓ Overt threats.

- ✓ Manipulative behaviour (for example: threatening to harm themselves in order to get a response to such an "emergency" in the form of contact).
- ✓ Sending written messages: letters, e-mails, graffiti, etc.
- ✓ The persistent sending of gifts.
- ✓ Defamation: The stalker often lies to others about the victim.
- ✓ "Objectification": The stalker derogates the victim reducing him/her to an object. This allows the stalker the ability to feel angry with the victim without experiencing empathy.

5) Friendly Neighbourhood

It would be easier to locate the person to monitor his/her friends rather than the relatives. The investigator's information dossier formed with our questionnaire in the appendices would help most of the information and commence the work.

If no relatives or known associates can be found or will talk, note the areas where the absconder was last known to be. Check with her landlord (if he/she rented) and with neighbours. Neighbours will often know where the subject has moved to maybe in certain area/locality, but enough information to aid in locating her. Also, check with former co-workers and bosses. You might present yourself as an old colleague or friend, but if you do, be sure you have enough details to pull it off. Check the withdrawal of money by ATM, the GPS location and the tower/CCTV footage to establish the absconder's movement. This would be covered more in the chapter for Missing Person in a digital manner.

6) Legal Permission for CDR/SDR

In order to obtain the access to the mobile data, there would be essential requirement of legal permission which can be in the form of FIR (First Information Report) reading the missing person. In many a case, one can obtain the court's permission too if reasons exists. One can also develop relationships with phone company personnel and paying them for these private records.

The police can also order CCTV footage on the departure trail of the absconder. Alternatively, CDR (Call Data Records) can give the details of his confidant who is in touch with him. The CDR would be able to give the information of his/her ip details which can be traced as covered in the training. SDR is called as Subscriber Data Records. The details in SDR contain the address details from the SIM issuing authority as per KYC (Know Your Customer).

7) Surveillance Types

There are three basic types of surveillance: moving, stationary, and foot. However, surveillance can start out as on type and change quickly to another. Therefore, you must be prepared for any type of surveillance when you set out to watch someone.

a) Moving Surveillance

Moving, or rolling, surveillance is often conducted in an automobile, but other common methods include bicycles, watercraft, aircraft, or trains. It can be exciting or alarming, depending on the Private Investigator. The first rule of moving surveillance is to not put yourself or other drivers in danger. If you lose the target and everyone does at one time or another, realize that you may pick him/her up later. If you don't, return another day. PIs consider it a point of pride to be able to stay with the target, but you can't develop that skill overnight. It takes a lot of practice to tail successfully, so give yourself a break in the beginning. Don't run red lights or stop signs or pull out in front of other drivers in order to stay with the subject.

It's important to stay one or two car lengths behind the subject vehicle, unless you're in heavy traffic where he might turn off, leaving you unable to follow safely. Also, be alert to every possible turn off or turn around, as you may need it at a moment's notice. If you are working alone, moving surveillance will be extremely difficult, but not impossible. Use your profile so that if you lose the subject, you can check out the areas he frequents and pick him up again.

A GPS device is useful for rolling surveillance. When you are in unfamiliar areas, it will help you navigate easily; if you become completely lost, it will get you back to a known location. Tracking devices are also helpful, but they are illegal in some states, so check your laws. With real-time tracking devices, you'll need to subscribe to a service. If you are working a divorce case or one where your client is the owner or co-owner of the car you are tailing, you might allow her to attach a tracking device. It can be argued, however, that she's doing this at your direction, and it could still be illegal. At any rate, it's always best to run anything like this by your attorney.

b) Stationary Surveillance

Stationery surveillance is difficult for many Private Investigators, mainly because of the sheer boredom that some feel when sitting for hours in a vehicle with nothing to do but stare at one location. Sometimes, however, it's the only way to obtain video of a subject who rarely exits his home.

Preparations

When you do stationary surveillance in winter, be careful of running your vehicle for warmth, as the exhaust may be apparent, much as warm breath on a cold day. Exhaust coming from a parked vehicle may draw the attention of an otherwise unsuspecting target and the neighbours. Some neighbourhoods are organized into neighbourhood watch sections. If you're parked in one of these, be prepared to provide a pretext for why you're sitting there.

Investigators have used the ruse of looking for a lost dog or cat, and have even printed bogus flyers to validate being in the area. However, this isn't recommended by experienced PIs. Someone who's out looking for a lost animal will be out looking, sometimes desperately. This won't be a believable ruse to most. Besides, some of the target's neighbours may have a soft spot, should they believe you, and may waste your time and energy by insisting on searching with you for your pet.

Some investigators enjoy stationary surveillance. They report feeling energized by the knowledge that, at any moment, the target may exit, requiring quick action in order to film her. They feel wound up, anticipating the moment when they get that difficult shot. It's a rush for them. It's what you're paid to do and so no imagining.

Neighbourhood Issues

Stationary surveillance is remaining in one location, which could include watching the subject from a parked car. in neighbourhoods is difficult. There are no good places to park. Sometimes, neighbours will allow you to sit in their driveway or in front of their house, usually because you've offered a plausible reason for wanting to be there. One investigator has been known to tell a female neighbour that he's watching a male cheating on his wife; he tells a male the investigation concerns a female cheating on her husband. Sometimes, the neighbour is sympathetic and will allow the surveillance vehicle in front of her house. Another investigator tells neighbours that she's received information that her spouse was seen in the neighbourhood during working hours and she's waiting to see where he goes. You might not as convincing, so choose a ruse that you can portray believably.

If police are called, don't lie to them. Tell them you're an investigator and ask for their help. Some will help, but some won't. If you know you'll be in an area ahead of time, call the station and inform them. It's not necessary to divulge the name or address of the target, however; you never know who knows whom. This is one reason it's beneficial to develop contacts in the department.

c) Foot Surveillance

Foot surveillance is usually undertaken by two or more individuals. Normally, one surveillant remains close to the target while the other stays at a greater distance. The second surveillant may follow the first on the same side of the street or travel on the opposite side. The positions of the surveillants are frequently changed, most commonly at road junctions. This requires that you be alert not only to those people behind you but also to those across the street and in front of you. If you see the same person more than once over a certain distance, even if that person is not seen continuously, surveillance may be suspected. Individuals who are alert to the people in their vicinity will eventually detect the same surveillant over a period of time.

The following are some guidelines for foot surveillance:

- Leave your vehicle quickly but unobtrusively
- Stay far behind that the target doesn't notice you
- Stay close enough that you don't lose the subject
- Avoid making eye contact with the target, but don't hide or make sudden movements
- Don't change hats or clothing unless the change totally alters your appearance
- Don't be afraid to shoot video using a very small camera or body cam
- Use store windows when available to observe target

Detecting Foot Surveillance

Some of the most effective methods for detecting foot surveillance are:

- Enquiring with incomplete or wrong information
- Stopping abruptly and looking to the rear
- Suddenly reversing your path.
- Stopping abruptly after turning a corner
- Watching reflections in shop windows or other reflective surfaces
- Entering a building and leaving immediately by another exit

- Walking slowly and then rapidly at intervals
- Dropping a piece of paper to see if anyone retrieves it
- Boarding or exiting a bus or train just before it starts
- Making sudden turns or walking around the block

8) Covert Cameras

Covert cameras can be used in many types of surveillances. The cameras can be placed on the dashboard or rear of the car or windows of your vehicle for streaming videos. After positioning it, the investigator can move away from the vehicle and allow the filming to continue. There are motion-activated cameras, to obviate the need to continuously monitoring or stopping and restarting.

The cameras are generally available in the ecommerce sites. One can choose a camera with longer battery life and zoom (digital zoom and optical zoom).

Cameras can also be worn on the investigators body or clothing. There are pen cameras, specs and button cameras too. The investigator can go anywhere and record anyone using these cameras without causing any type of suspicion.

9) Night-time Surveillance

While following a vehicle, it is a good idea to put a tape on the tail light of the subject's car for easy identification during the day time and also during the night time surveillance. The private investigator should try to drive in a manner that he/she is not visible to the subject. One is expected to avoid overtaking and then falling back and again overtaking the subject as it can cause suspicion.

10) Surveillance Vehicles

The private investigator can kit up his/her vehicle (2-wheeler or 4-wheeler) for the purpose of undertaking any surveillance. Alternatively, one can also consider using auto or any hired cab to increase the anonymity in following the subject. The vehicle should be comfortable for day or night surveillance and also if it is raining/snowing.

11) Digital and Electronic Surveillance

The technical driven surveillance encompasses digital and electronic surveillance. In the digital surveillance, the subject is monitored by his digital presence by means of his GPS (global positioning system) and tower location. Whereas the electronic surveillance, include audio and video surveillance methodology. These types of surveillance are illegal though, but it can be a good source of the subject's presence in stealth. The illegality aspect can be diluted by riding on the police complaint. For illegal activities and accused, the illegality aspect is debatable.

Bugs, Taps, and Wiretaps

The term bug refers to a microphone or camera placed somewhere in a room which picks up conversations and transmits them wirelessly or through connecting cables, to a receiver outside of the room. A tap usually refers to a device that has intercepted the lines of your phone and is recording the conversations. Many taps for this requirement are available freely on the ecommerce sites.

A wiretap placed on your phone by law enforcement is neither of these things. When a police wiretap is operated, the mobile company provides an extension of your line to the particular office of the monitoring agency. This means that when the phone rings at your place, it also rings at the monitoring office or the designated place for the recording purpose. To put a wiretap, the phone company will have to be provided with the written authority letter by the police/legal agency. The interested parties may also initiate to wiretap the conversations illegally by either working independently to take a tapping of the phone line (s) or get it done by greasing the palms of the linesman. The requirement of wiretapping can be based on either recording the conversation or just knowing the numbers called or both. To know the numbers dialled, one can put pin registers and capture the numbers dialled on the outgoing calls. Trap and trace devices, however capture numbers dialled on the incoming calls.

Children's Phone Monitoring

The private investigator can install some of the several applications for GPS and social media activity monitoring. It is very easy to find where your children is located or has been moving on any particular date and time. This topic is covered adequately during the online sessions of our Private Investigator's Course.

Nine

Devices for Audio & Video Bugging

The private investigator is a business to devote time and undertake skill based investigations in information domain. There are specific tools to uncover the evidence. Using a computer system preferably a laptop, one can take on surveillance. This chapter will concentrate on audio and video equipment necessary to the Private Investigator's goal of acquiring information.

1) Video Equipment

Video equipment is perhaps the most important of all the tools in the investigator's bag. Nothing convinces more than video. It trumps eyewitness testimony, audio recordings, and any other type of evidence as far as believability and reliability.

a) Surveillance Camcorder

Camcorders are available in many types. Smaller the camcorder, better it is. New camcorders are remarkably small and can be easily concealed.

There are certain things you want in your camcorder. The recommended features will give you an idea of what's important to the work of a PI:

- **Image stabilization.** This is important in keeping your video steady.
- **Time/date stamp.** This is essential for film that you want to enter into evidence.
- **Zoom lens.** Some cameras have 35X-45X optical zoom—the longer the better because you won't need to get as close to your target.
- **Night vision feature.** This is a low lux feature that allows you film at night.

- **Auto focus.** With auto focus, you can concentrate on the target instead of the camera focus; it also enables you to shoot quickly without needing to make any changes.
- **Storage and Wi-Fi connectivity.** This feature would be of help to clear the camera storage space and record the activities for a longer period of time.

b) Camcorder Accessories

The Private Investigator should the necessary accessories of his camcorder like extra batteries, foldable stand/tripods for the stationary surveillance. One can place the tripod in the rear of his/her vehicle or near the front window/dashboard as convenient.

PI is expected to have accessories to include extra batteries and foldable tripod. Tripods are invaluable during stationary surveillance.

c) Still Cameras

Photo snaps are taken by the still cameras. These days the mobiles too come with great features. One can have a 35mm or a digital camera with at least 24-megapixel capability. One should be able to store the images in a pen drive or the laptop or any other storage media.

As with camcorders, be sure that your digital camera has the highest power of optical zoom if possible. Optical zoom is considered more important than the digital zoom. An optical zoom gives you enhanced clarity and a greater ability to enlarge the picture while retaining much of that clarity.

d) Binoculars

Binoculars are one of the essential pieces of surveillance equipment. They range in price and size, just as so many other items do. You won't need those huge Coast Guard looking binoculars, but neither do you want a tiny pair that is inferior in quality.

Powers of the binocular should be more than 12X50. A high aperture will give one a wider view. The wider field of view also ensures that you'll miss less of any quick movements made by your target. The 10X and higher will provide more detail and better viewing for longer distances and open terrain. Binocular sizes are expressed with two numbers: 7x35, 10x50, etc. The first number is the magnification (or power), the second is the aperture, or diameter of the objective (front) lenses in millimetres. For example, 7x35 binoculars provide 7x power magnification and have 35mm objective lenses.

There are two principal types of prisms in a binocular: roof and Porro. The glass elements in a roof prism are in line with one another, making roof-prism binoculars straight and easier to hold. Porro prisms have the glass elements offset from one another, and can provide greater depth of field and a wider field of view compared to similar roof prism models. This is accomplished by folding the light path, which shortens the length, spreading the objectives farther apart. One may consider the cheaper alternative of a monocular which can be connected with a mobile to directly record or zoom in mobile handsets.

e) Wireless Versus Wired Cameras

You might ask about wireless cameras, thinking they have the same capabilities as wired cameras. They do, but there have always been drawbacks to wireless transmission.

Problems with Wireless Transmission

- Other wireless devices can and do interfere with wireless transmission. Devices such as portable phones, some cable connections, microwaves, and other items can render wireless cameras almost useless.
- Wireless depends, usually, on line of sight
- Transmission is limited to a fixed distance between transmitter and camera receiver. Usually, the distance is very short. Only law

enforcement personnel are allowed to use wireless transmission that extends far enough for a backup team to be inconspicuous.

f) Mobile Covert Cameras

Only a few years ago, if investigators wanted to wear a covert body camera, it entailed finding a way to conceal a not-so-small video recorder on his person and inconspicuously run wires to a camera, such as a pen, watch, or spectacles. Due to this, every shirt, jacket, and pair of jeans or slacks contained a hole threading a line to the covert camera. It is much different today; it's easier and less visible to wear covet gadgets.

The Private Investigators generally roams around recording, checking the victim's room, common areas, living room, and kitchens. In cases of the abused spouse, recorded evidence are rarely challenged.

2. Audio Equipment

Audio equipment refers to devices that reproduce, record, or process sound. This includes microphones, radio receivers, AV receivers, stealth audio recorders, amplifiers, mixing consoles, effects units, loudspeakers and similar gadgets.

A collection of audio gadget should be available with the private investigator. There is a great requirement of recording audio of the subjects and the requests are increasing day by day. There may be no need for video at times, or may not want to invest in stealth cameras. In this case, the private investigator can go in for voice activated audio recorders or listeners.

a) Audio Bugs

Audio bugs are small devices requiring either a continuous power source or a long battery life. These are generally hidden in the electric sockets or telephone so that the power source is continuously maintained.

b) Wired Microphones

In earlier days, these types of powered microphones used to be laid either behind the wall plaster or hidden behind devices to feed the voice continuously to the other party.

c) Telephone Bugs

Bugging a telephone instrument was earlier easier to record the calls of the telephone user. Later on the tapping of wire was resorted to tap the conversations.

#Ten

Missing Persons

1) What is Skip Tracing?

Skip tracing is the art of locating people who have gone missing/absconded. Skip tracing means to find the details of the person in question. Investigations of missing persons are usually known as domestic cases, although some missing persons have nothing to do with domestic situations. Investigating missing persons is very common type of case for which a private investigator could be hired. This section outlines conventional skip tracing, an investigative specialty that is about locating people who've skipped out on something or someone. Skip tracing is used in missing persons and absconding cases as per relevance.

Overview of Skip Tracing

Skip tracing investigations can be a lucrative for our trained investigators, especially if investigators cultivate relationships with banks, legal professionals, insurance companies and loan companies. There are many resources you can use to help you find a missing or absconding person.

Around 80 percent of people reported as missing have been found to be absconding.

Some hide after taking loans from banks/people, families, or spouses. Others could be hiding to avoid harassments of any likely revelations which may surface sooner or later. Others may disappear due to psychological or health problems. Many of these skips return or are located. Some adults walk out of their homes or workplaces and never return. If no physical or emotional illness is present, and no suspicion of wrongdoing surrounds their departure, it may not be reported. The disappearance of less known people, drug addicted, and the physically, emotionally, or psychologically challenged may not be reported. The investigator has to be cautious while handling cases of missing children as they can't manage themselves and are likely to fall prey to unsocial elements and get exploited physically, mentally or emotionally.

Many children are abducted by parent or caretakers who used to know them very well. But abduction is the term which is not acceptable legally. Such children may still be in danger of emotional exploitation or physical abuse.

2) Person Not Intentionally Missing

The first type of missing person is the one who doesn't know anyone is looking for him/her. Although the person may actually not be hiding, but the subject would have realised that no one is caring for him/her and could have left his/her home to spend time with his/her close associate of the past or present. Other reasons which could lead to such elopement could be any of the following.

- An old love or friend
- Runaway children or adolescents with little or unconcerned family/relations.
- A person of interest or witness to crime could also change his/her surrounding intentionally.
- Hospitalisation, memory loss, head injury or death owing to accidents, etc should also be explored.

3) Absconders

This skip is in hiding and determined to stay missing. As such, he/she poses a challenge. In such case/s, the location of hiding and or new job/work, etc can lead the conventional detective to seek information from the last friendly contacts, police case information if available. These cases are best investigated by a Cyber Detective and the methodology is covered in Part 3 in detail. Reasons leading to absconding or intentionally missing could be as under:

- Bail bond absconders
- Overdue payments, loans or heavy debts without any source of income.
- Runaway children or adolescents to attractions like fantasy or infatuation.
- Tenant skips: payments of commercial and residential rent in the absence of work/source of income
- Persons wanted for the purpose of a likely legal/court case stress or to avoid other legal actions
- To avoid legal directive/obligation of alimony and child support

4) Skip Tracing in the Digital World

An investigator sitting at a computer all day, finding everything he needs to locate skips is not likely to yield result. The Internet is a wonderful tool for absconders, but it is unlikely to lead you to success. There are still many records that aren't online or show information only for recent years. Some types of information may never be collected and distributed in an online database. Therefore, you must know where to look for the subject. This type of skip tracing in the digital world will be covered in detail later in Part 3.

Missing Children and Adolescents

The missing children cases can be reported to police apart from investigations by hired private investigators. Since the children are highly vulnerable to exploitation, the cases are handled at high priority and with care to obviate any likely harm by the kidnappers.

Stranger Versus Known Abductor

Most investigators who search for abducted children no longer make a great distinction between the stranger abductor and the known abductor. One reason is that children and even parents have difficulty making that distinction. Who is the stranger? Is the clerk at the local store? Is it the insurance salesman, the maintenance man, or the servant or the driver?

It is generally seen that the abductor has been either known or has been stalking the child or the family for some time before resorting to such crimes. The previous worker/delivery man or the revengeful person could easily take the child in pseudo confidence and abduct the child. There could be persons closer to families who could be the most likely abductors of children. The category of such abductors could be medical assistants, mechanics, plumbers, electricians or school staff including the drivers or the care taker. The abduction of the child could be because of the sexual exploitation, ransom and or property issues. The child in anyway is at a greater risk of life.

Missing Adolescents

Adolescent age-groups fall between children and adults. This age bracket may slightly vary for different sects and generally may fall between 13 years to 18 years. During this period the person's physical, mental and emotional states make them highly vulnerable to wrong decisions as they could be infatuated beyond the real world. In general, the adolescent goes missing in search of the gratification which they think can be provided by their friend/relative or even unknown. They can be also lured in the name of job with comfort and career growth. These aspects may lead to factual revelations if investigated.

Involuntarily Missing Adolescents

Adolescents go missing for numerous reasons, but recent years have seen an increase in adolescents who leave after meeting someone they have made contact with on the social media. These adolescents don't always intend to leave home permanently, but when they find that the abductor could put them in danger, it is generally late. Some adolescents are sold or used as sex slaves, some are released after differing stages of abuse, and some are never seen alive again.

The world holds many dangers. The attraction to materialistic life style like alcohol, drugs, freedom to live and false promise to settle down with career growth may obfuscate the victim's thinking capacity and difficult to recognize the lurking dangers. The private investigators with computer skills may be able to solve the cases as is done by few experts trained by us in our Private Investigator's course.

Voluntarily Missing or Runaway Adolescents

The present times where the missing child or adolescent is most likely to be on social media and getting their new handset details, new contact numbers and or email ids can lead the private investigator to vital clues. On the other hand, the police can get their tower location to pinpoint their city and the area where they are staying.

Eleven

Abuse Investigations

Abuse often has nothing to do with the reason someone is missing, but in some cases, it's a direct factor. Also, because many missing children are abused by their abductors or leave home because of abuse, these categories are discussed together. Any abuse is reprehensible, but child and elder abuse are especially repugnant. These populations are vulnerable targets and must be protected by those responsible for their care.

1) Child Abuse Investigations

The demand for investigating abuse cases, especially child abuse cases, has grown in recent years. Many theories as to whether abuse has increased or is simply being reported come to light. Victims have historically been ashamed of revealing abuse because they felt they were somehow to blame, but things are now different and more legally conscious. Many experts feel that the media has been influential in highlighting the scope of abuse, but critics argue that they have been responsible for creating an unwarranted nationwide fear of abusers. An uncomfortable truth is that law enforcement personnel who work on such cases are astounded at the numbers of abusers encountered in a single operation. They don't feel that the media or anyone else is overstating the danger, and they urge that more media awareness and community education is warranted. Further time and research may reveal the truth of this, but for now, it is incumbent upon everyone to be aware of these abusers and be knowledgeable of the best means for be aware of these abusers and be knowledgeable of the best means for protecting children from them.

The Private Investigator should be aware of the utilities of the portals for reporting the crimes and child abuse. The national portals in India for reporting are:

- National Crime Records Bureau:

  https://ncrb.gov.in/

- National Commission for Protection of Child Rights:

  https://ncpcr.gov.in/

The common types of child abuse could be physical, emotional, and sexual. Child abuse is considered as a criminal offence. Physical and sexual abuse inhibits children growth. The investigator may need to take with him a lady for counselling and moral boosting of the child for a comforting communication, and more so, if the victim is a female.

2) Recognizing Physical Abuse of Children and Adolescents

There are many signs that a child is being abused or neglected. Indications include the following behaviours by the abuser:

- Expressing anguish to the child like clumsiness and derogatory comments
- Depriving the child of his/her prestige and biased behaviour towards him/her.
- Expressing that the child is useless and worthless.
- Not encouraging good deeds of the child and always discouraging him/her.
- Not being sympathetic towards the child if hurt or ill.
- Doesn't pay attention to the growth of the child.
- Exposing the child to immoral behaviour like serving drinks or like slave.

- Always remains around the child for the fear of his/her disclosure.

The abused child develops the following types of complex:

- Change in personality, temperament, appetite, or school performance.
- Sad and gloomy appearance and subdued personality.
- Physical or mental exploitation signs.
- Prone to sexual harassments by anyone.

Speaking to the child in isolation can reveal many facts if given the confidence.

3) Recognizing Emotional Abuse in a Child or Adolescent

Emotional abuse leads a child or adolescent to physical exploitation. The suspect generally expresses extraordinary concern towards such children. Expensive presents, dresses or toys become the modus operandi of many suspects.

It is generally seen that the victims of sexual abuse generally try to stay aloof and their performance in education and other fields drops significantly. The child finds it easy to lie or steal petty but attractive stuffs.

4) Hidden Cameras and Child Abuse

It is not easy to find evidence of child abuse even if the child shows signs of abuse. In such a case, audio or video bugging of the suspected area where the physical abuse is more likely can reveal the facts.

5) The Paedophile

Paedophiles mean attraction of elders towards the children. The innocence and physical growth with the emotional attraction towards opposite sex are generally exploited by the grown up men and women alike. The police or the well wishers are hardly available to investigate such cases and hence the role of the private investigator.

6) Relationship Abuse

Most of the victims feel normal about such abuse because they have been subjected to the abusive relationship for longer period of time. If the victim has been living in such abusive environment, they start considering the events as a normal and may not realise the fact that it can be termed as abuse.

The longer the victim stays in the abusive environment, it becomes so normal to them and this fact gives the abuser more courage to increase the abuse. In such a case, it may become difficult for the victim to leave such situation. Similarly, violence can also increase gradually that the abused becomes conditioned to accept it until it rises to an unacceptable or alarming level.

Studies reveal that males generally never report abuse. Self-report studies have shown that the main reason for this is because males are ashamed to report abuse at the hand of a woman. Teenagers, similarly feel that this must be the open society norm or being broadminded.

Since it's difficult to prove, without proof, it remains just an argument. In this situation, males and females alike will turn to a private investigator in hopes of gathering evidence to prove their claim. Private Investigators often deploy hidden cameras to catch the abuser in the act. This eliminates most of the abuser's defence, as crime is available as evidence.

a) Relationship Abuse

Abuse is one of a serious crime. The examples of abuse could be relationship abusers, threaten, verbal abuse, emotional abuse, physical abuse involving pulling hair, pushing, throwing, slapping, pinching, choking, squeezing or smooching, or attacking the person with some objects. Abuse generally starts with minor injury whether it is mentally or physically and later increases slowly and the victim often gets used to accept the threat or major injury.

b) Teen Dating Abuse

Dating abuse generally is very common. Teens are highly at risk as they are the most vulnerable due to inexperience and lack of power or shame. Teens at times consider it as possessiveness, jealousy and even physical abuse as proof of love.

According to research performed in March 2006 by Teenage Research Unlimited (TRU), the following numbers tell the disturbing tale:

- One in five teens in a relationship report being slapped, hit, or pushed
- One in three girls in a relationship report concern that they would be physically hurt
- One in four teens in a serious relationship report concern that partner has tried to keep them from family and friends and pressured them to spend time only with the partner
- One in three girls between the ages of sixteen and eighteen report that sex is expected in a relationship
- Half of these girls experiencing sexual pressure report that they fear the relationship will end if sex isn't provided
- Nearly one in four girls reported continuing further sexually than they wanted because of pressure

Vigilance and surveillance is the best method of determining how someone is treated. One can follow the teen and her suspect. With hidden cameras or audio bugs in their place of living or where they spend time, it is possible to gather evidence.

When it comes to investigation, the Private Investigator is expected to discuss the subject with the teachers, relatives, neighbours, friends and whoever is generally present in the area the victim visits.

The installed CCTV in the areas can be sought with the approval of the authorities. Alternatively, own wireless cameras can be planted apart from tipping the staff around the surroundings like cafe shops, cafeterias, etc.

c) Elder Abuse

Elder abuse also goes unreported for the sole reason that the elders generally prefer peace and feel that such abuse may end sooner or later. There are elders who could be attracted to children or some could be themselves vulnerable to exploitation by others either emotionally or physically. This type of investigation should be undertaken in a very cordial manner without any suspicion. It could be recommended to record the environment and stream either live or play it to the applicant to show how safe the elder is. The concern here is to establish whether the elder is in a hygienic environment or not. The treatment given to the elders can be recorded as evidence and sorted out. In India, generally the elders stay with the children and are less likely to be a victim of abuse, but during the day time, when most of the members are out on duty/job, the elders could be stilled watched over by streaming hidden cameras to ensure their safety from any likely outsiders or known persons. In homes where the in-laws are living, the treatment meted out to the elders may be investigated best by the audio or video bugging devices.

The fee charged to investigate any elder care varies depending on the complexity and distance involved. The investigation is generally easy and recording is also not difficult.

Twelve

Background Checks

Many areas related to private investigation are becoming growth industries. Some of these may not be considered private investigation to the public, but they fall under the broad heading of Private Investigator's work. Several of the most popular specialties will be discussed in this chapter, but there are many more.

The business of providing pre-employment and background checks to businesses and the public alike is growing by leaps and bounds. Aside from cost, the most important aspect of a background/pre-employment check is accuracy and completeness. Almost anyone can apply to online systems that claim to supply full background and criminal history reports. However, there are problems with many of these. One of the valuable evidence is hampered view limited access to complete records that are updated often in the state repositories. The methodology of background checks can be broadly classified in two categories: conventional and cyber.

1) Background/Pre-Employment Search

If you are going to run background/pre-employment searches, it's helpful to know who purchases them.

a) An insurance company may purchase background information on someone to be sure she isn't a serial complainant and that she isn't double-dipping or receiving compensation from other departments.

b) The Investigator may have to procure the background checks on behalf of their own clients, especially those involved in divorce, personal injury, lawsuit, child custody, and criminal or civil cases.

c) Business owners purchase pre-employment checks before hiring employees.

d) Individuals often want to check backgrounds for personal reasons, most commonly for information about those they're dating, their fiancés, birth parents, siblings, or children, or for locating an old friend or high school sweetheart.

Sometimes information checks are ordered to search for new information and to verify information already in the client's possession, such as that provided on job applications.

2) The Internet and Background Checks

Employers and investigators alike have added a strategy to the traditional background check. They use various search engines, as well as social networking sites such as Spokeo, YouTube, instagram and Facebook apart from different trackers to identify the subject by their mobile numbers and email addresses.

What many searchers find on these sites is disturbing and revealing in most cases. Very often, the clean-cut professional appears on his site as someone else entirely. Revealing pictures and the discussion of controversial subjects can damage job applicants. When something is posted on the Internet, the poster loses all control of it. For the PI performing a background search, checking these sites can throw light on a different aspect of the applicant.

It is customary to build up a character related profile from the likes and events where the subject has ventured out. The types of friends would also determine his/her taste and interests. The associations generally give likes to their loves/close friends in all their posts and the same would imply their virtual closeness. The photographs/post would also indicate the likely places they have been visiting or likely to visit. Such profiles are generally locked but the investigator would have to enter their profiles through their friends or through their pseudo profiles.

Thirteen

Gathering Evidences

Gathering evidences is an important skill for a successful Private Investigator. The evidences gathered should be in line with the objective of the case in hand. The police and the Private Investigator may collect physical evidence at the crime scene. This may include taking photographs, measurements, fingerprints, blood samples, and taking any objects that may be related to the crime. Each bit of evidence must then be properly recorded and documented as exhibits. Some evidence that is not admissible on its own may be admissible in conjunction with other types of evidence. Evidences are generally known to be of following types:-

- **Analogical Evidence**: The comparative or correlated and implied evidences are covered under analogical evidence. It is not a strong evidence to prove the point.
- **Anecdotal Evidence:** Anecdotal evidences are considered unreliable and sketchy as it is related to anecdotes. It can be quoted in conjunction with other evidences.
- **Character Evidence:** Character Evidence can be quoted with examples depicting either a loose character or of high moral character. This is also not considered a direct evidence, but can impress the court to increase the scope of liberal/stronger view depending on the case in hand. It denotes intent and the motive of the subject.
- **Circumstantial Evidence:** This pertains to the facts and figures to prove the arguments. This should highlight the circumstances based on which the subject's mental frame made him/her to take particular step/s.

- **Demonstrative Evidence:** This type of evidence carries lot of value as the produced document is considered to be demonstrative in nature to prove a fact. It could be photographs, narratives, diaries, logs, tickets, receipts, etc.
- **Digital Evidence:** Evidence of this type could be audio,video, email, screenshot, image files, forensics report of PC/Laptops or mobiles, etc. Since these are the digital evidences, it would be required to produce with the 65B of the Indian Evidence Act. While producing the evidences, hashing of the evidence is considered mandatory in the court to prove integrity of the original file.
- **Direct Evidence:** This type of evidence encompasses testimony of the witness, his/her statements, affidavit, etc. The description of the eye witness is considered a game changer as it is itself a proof.
- **Documentary Evidence:** It includes letters, wills, plans or even the diary notes, and may include drawings, images, audio/video clips too.
- **Exculpatory Evidence:** Any evidence that is favourable to the defendant in a criminal trial is considered exculpatory. Evidence showing that the defendant is not guilty is considered exculpatory.
- **InculpatoryEvidence:** Evidence favourable to the prosecution is termed as inculpatory.
- **Forensics Evidence:** Forensic evidence is scientific evidence like DNA, fingerprints or ballistics reports which can establish a person's involvement or innocence. This evidence is considered to be strong and reliable.
- **Physical Evidence:** Physical evidence from the crime scene in the form of an object, such as a personal clothing, firearm, leftover objects, sharp objects, fingerprints, rope purportedly used to strangle someone, etc from a crime scene, is considered to be physical evidence. Physical evidence is also known as "real" or "material"

evidence. It can be presented in court as an exhibit of a physical object, captured in still or moving images, described in text, audio or video or referred to in documents. Objects will need to be kept in specially made evidence bags.

- **Prima Facie Evidence:** The evidence based on presumption may initially be indicative of a particular act till such time it is negated or rebutted during the proceedings.
- **Statistical Evidence:** Evidence that uses numbers (or statistics) to support a position is called statistical evidence. This type of evidence is based on research or polls. It is not a direct evidence but indicative type.
- **Testimonial Evidence:** Statements under oath by witness in either verbal or written or by an affidavit is considered as testimonial evidence.

The evidences could be any of the following types:

a) Photographic evidence

b) Statements of connected people

c) Audio recordings

d) Wi-Fi and Bluetooth pairing

e) Emails

f) Job applications

g) Credit/Debit card bills

h) Bank accounts and ATM

PART 3

Manoeuvre in the Digital Space

Fourteen

Cyber Skills and Methodology

1) Indian IT Act

The Indian IT Act was first introduced in the year 2000 with amendments and alterations in 2008 and later. The IT acts are comprehensive and certain acts have been altered or amplified too. A list of the 'Information Technology Acts' are tabulated below for easy referral.

SECTION COMES UNDER I.T ACT 2000 AMMENDED

Sec	Description
43	Penalty and compensation for damage to computer, computer system, etc
65	Tampering with computer source documents
66	Computer related offenses
66a Rem-oved	This sec used to deal with sending or posting offensive messages by any communicating medium, but has been removed and can be dealt in defamatory cases if applicable
66c	Punishment for identity theft
66d	Punishment for cheating by impersonation by using computer resource
66e	Punishment for violation of privacy
66f	Cyber terrorism
67	Punishment for publishing or transmitting obscene material in

	electronic form
67a	Punishment for publishing or transmitting of material containing sexually explicit act, etc. In electronic form
67b	Punishment for publishing or transmitting of material depicting children in sexually explicit act, etc. In electronic form
69	Powers to issue directions for interception or monitoring or decryption of any information through any computer resource
69a	Power to issue directions for blocking for public access of any information through any computer resource
69b	Power to authorize to monitor and collect traffic data or information through any computer resource for cyber security
71	Penalty for misrepresentation for obtaining license/certificate from certifying authority
72	Breach of confidentiality and privacy
72a	Punishment for disclosure of information in breach of lawful contract
73	Penalty for publishing electronic signature certificate false in certain particulars
74	Publication for fraudulent purpose
75	Act to apply for offence or contraventions committed outside india
77a	Compounding of offences.
77b	Offences with three years imprisonment to be cognizable
78	Power to investigate offences

2) Crime Scene Investigation and Cyber Forensics

The following points are to be borne in mind during any Crime Scene and Cyber Forensics Investigations:-

a) If a Computer System is on, one may carry out snap forensics or just shut down the system (without switching off the power) so as to gather the volatile data.

b) If a Computer System is off, the CPU/laptop should be removed off the cables and collected (without switching it on)

c) If the Computer System is in crashed state, the Master Boot Record could be corrupted and in such a case, the HDD should be removed and taken in custody.

d) Have necessary tools to handle locked computer systems, Cyber Forensics, hashing tools which can run from pen drives and save the results on the pen drive.

e) Do not forget to collect the storage drives/devices from the crime scene and label it for record purposes.

f) Obtain all possible passwords of devices collected/confiscated.

g) Initiate chain of custody of devices.

h) Obtain appropriate written permissions for cyber forensics if the private investigator has been requested to investigate.

3) Criminal Profiling

Criminal profiling signifies getting the additional contact details like contact numbers, email addresses, social media accounts, place of work, business, etc besides his/her residential address/location. This is generally achieved by offensive as well as passive means. Offensive methodology can be taken legally only after a police complaint either on request by the police or by the victim if police is not able to get the details. Passive methodology can be used to get the details from digital means coupled with extraction methodology for additional details. The profiling is also undertaken for missing and absconding persons. While we understand that the police generally can get the details of additional mobile numbers by getting the Call Data Records (CDR), Subscriber Data Records (SDR) and International Mobile Equipment Identity (IMEI) request to the Internet Service Provider (ISP), but if the fraudster/hacker/absconder changes his/her handset, the details of IMEI becomes futile. The new handset would have a different IMEI number.

General Profiling

The general profiling comprises of offensive profiling and passive profiling. It is undertaken for missing, absconding persons or criminals. It is important to know the interests or hobbies of the subject for easy profiling. The methodology for undertaking general profiling can be formulated taking into account the following enlisted aspects:

a) Handset Details of the subject: Can be obtained by trying to login gmail/google with the connected mobile/email id for any user.

b) Alternate emails of the subject: Can be obtained by getting the clue from the recovery of email and then by social engineering or guessing the missing parameters and confirming the findings with repeat recover method to establish the new email ids.

c) Details of the changed handsets can be established by the recovery mode of step (a).

d) Phishing email with spoofing techniques combined can help get more credentials of the established fraudster/criminal.

e) Profile search on social media: The profile search confirmation can be obtained from the available social media search by trying to create the login id with the help of available/new contact details (email or mobile number)

f) The sites which would give one the details are naukri.com, linkedin.com, indeed.com, quicker.com, olx.com, justdial.com, google.com, facebook.com, instagram.com, etc. Thereafter, one needs to search for the connected mobile numbers and email addresses and work on alternate numbers/email addresses.

g) One can also search about the person on Gpay, PayTm, amazon sites.

The methodologies of offensive, active, passive profiling and social engineering are enumerated as under:

Offensive Profiling

Offensive profiling is considered illegal and unethical. It involves getting information of the subjects by means of phishing, social engineering tactics. The victim is sent either a link or convinced to install certain applications which make them vulnerable to data/information loss. This is undertaken only if the cyber/police or legal request for finding the details of certain criminals who are trying to evade the law. How does one undertake offensive profiling? One can send phishing/grabbing links by email, sms or whatsapp to the victim and know their credentials or the geographical ip address. By sending the subject a phishing link, one can grab his/her credentials which can be used to login in his social media accounts. Once the password is obtained for the subject's email, the investigator/profiler adds another created email id in the forwarding mail tab under the settings tab to continue reading the emails even if the subject changes his/her password.

Passive Profiling

Passive Profiling is also illegal and unethical but with a police complaint along with the victim's request, one can find the information available on the digital space to supplement the ongoing police investigation. In this type of profiling, one can find the no. of email ids, profiles, mobile numbers. Most of the social media sites, one can either search the profiles by the subject's user id, profile names, mobiles or email ids. If this fails, one can try to find out if the mobile numbers or the emails are registered or not. One can either go to the recovery mode or try to register with the subject's mobile or email id. The site would either take you to the recovery page or similar hints implying that the subject is already registered on that social media.

Active Profiling

In active profiling, the investigator calls the subject to confuse the person to give the code/OTP for logging or snatching away the subject's profile of whatsapp, facebook, etc and then change the credentials. This is also unethical and illegal but can be tried to obtain the detailed information of the subject's profile. Example of this type of profiling is by calling the subject that his/her account is being used from two locations and the fact can be verified only by sending the OTP to the user's mobile numbers. The caller expresses himself/herself to be from the company/social media head office. This method is generally used for targeting subjects of different countries whose information can be utilised for the national cause. One can also obtain access to the control panel of the website hosted by the subject and add another created email id for continuous access to the business emails.

Social Engineering

Social engineering is an art wherein one can get more information about the subject by well crafted questions. The questions will need to be broader and generic so as to get a confirmed response. This methodology is generally used to get the area where the subject is currently located. Besides, the wireless network connected with the subject, information of router and service provider's information can easily compromise the network and provide entry into it.

4) Hacking by Links

Shortening of URL has got advantage as well as disadvantage. The main advantage being easy to share the shorten links instead of cumbersome long links. But since the original website is hidden, the links can lead a victim to malicious site as well. Some known urlshortners are explained below:-

a) Bitly<bitly.com>

Bitly offers a free and enterprise version of their URL shortening service. No signup necessary but creating an account allows you to manage links quickly and change the URL from the link http://bit.ly/Jhc38q to http://bit.ly/Intelligent. You can only use keywords that other people have not taken, though.

b) TinyURL

A simple shortener that requires no sign-up and allows users to customize the keyword. The service is free to use, but there is no analytics.

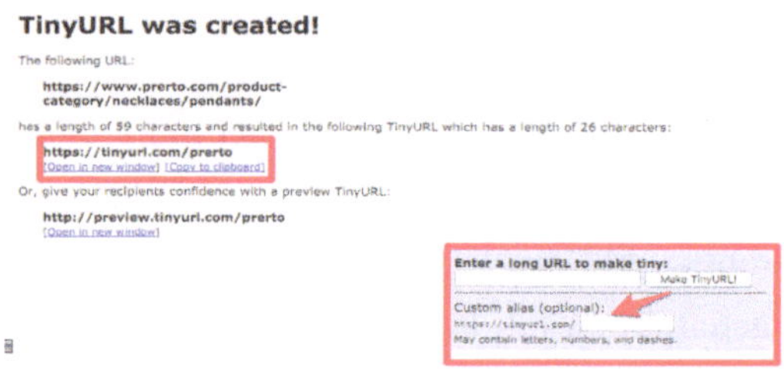

c) Tiny.cc

Tiny.cc is a popular and free service that can log basic statistics for each short URL. Tiny.cc also allows you to create a custom URL.

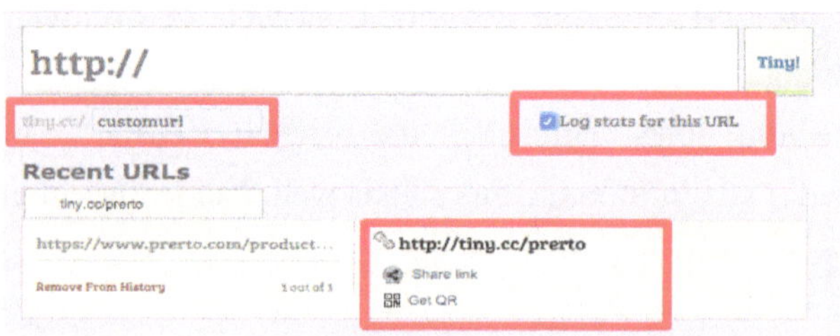

d) LiveChat URL shortener<https://www.livechatinc.com/url-shortener/>

This dominant URL shortener is a free link shortener that offers a unique feature – built-in URL builder that lets you tag your links with UTM parameters.

Also, it allows you to customize your short URL string, save the links you've shortened and track number of clicks they generated (the last two requires login with your Facebook account).

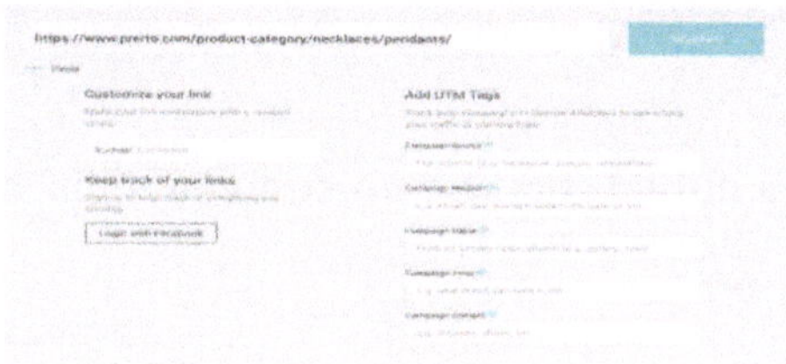

e) is.gd

A simple and very short URL is.gd also allows you to customize your short URL. No sign up required. You can log statistics from their links.

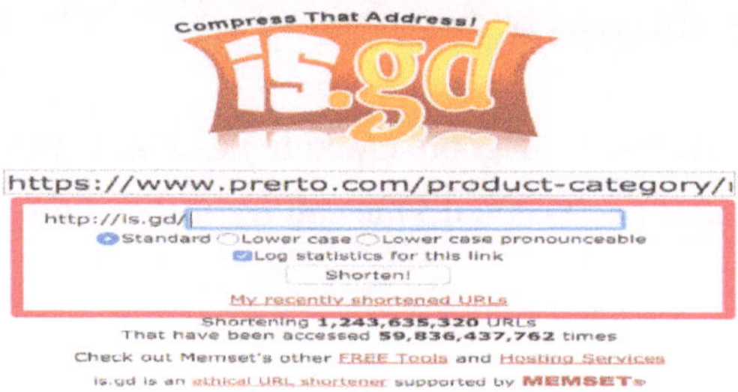

f) soo.gd

Free and easy to use link shortener that allows you to customize the suffix of the URL. However, there is no analytics.

g) s2r.co

This service offers no statistics and no customization. However, no sign up required.

Premium URL Shortners

The previous services do a good enough job but if you're looking for something extra and professional, one can try some of the following: -

h) clicky.me

Clicky.me is integrated with Clicky Web Analytics, giving you a world of analytics that many others don't offer. Clicky.me is designed specifically for sharing links to a website you are tracking with Clicky. You must sign up for Clicky Web Analytics. It requires a paid account too.

i) budurl.com

BudURL is more for brands and businesses. It offers extensive tracking and managing features in its paid plans that start at $24/mo. However, at $24/mo it also allows you to use a custom domain. Sign up required.

j) bc.vc

Another service that pays you for linking. They promise that you can make more than $4.00/1000 visitors, real-time statistics, and family-safe ads. Minimum payouts start at $10. No customization.

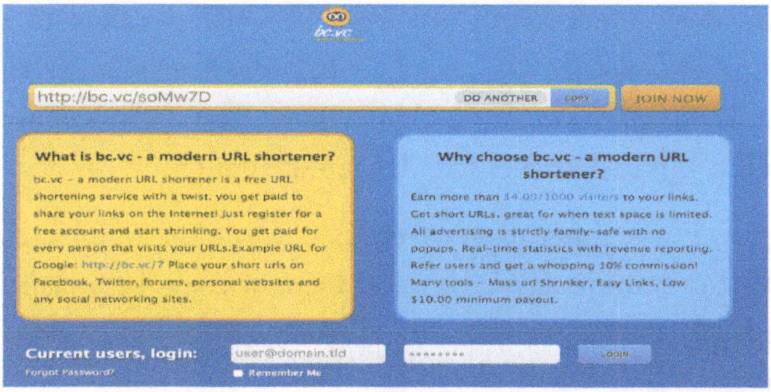

There are many url shortners coming up and some of the old ones are fading out of service.

Expanding Shortened URL

The shortend urls can be decoded into the original url in many cases. Following links would take you to the site where one needs to put the shortened link. The link expanders are more and in due course of time the present links could fade away from service too.

- http://checkshorturl.com/
- http://www.getlinkinfo.com/
- https://linkexpander.com/

5) Legitimate looking Links

With emerging social engineering tactics, it's quite common and simple to hack someone's credentials and personal information just by sending a link. Also, these links are quite simple to spoof and manipulate to lure the target in the name of a legitimate link. These links can be used in many ways depending upon the information to be collected. It could just be a simple link which captures the IP address of the person clicking it or a sophisticated password stealing link which grabs the credentials of social media accounts.

Also, one doesn't necessarily use specific tools or Linux to generate these kinds of links. In the example below we will understand how simple it is to make an IP grabbing link. The following website is basically is a URL shortener with IP capture option.

www.grabify.link – After opening the site, it will ask for an URL as an input. We can provide any URL over there; it could be a malicious site or a normal legitimate website. Upon generating a short URL, it may look likehttps://grabify.link/T6EUI2

Whosoever clicking on the link will be redirected to the website that we mentioned during generating the link. Upon clicking the above link, the IP address along with User-Agent and network provide will be captured.

Now this IP can be used to track the person or further process the information gathering stage. Apart from these simple IP capturing links, personal information and credentials too can be captured via the links.

Date/Time	IP Address	Country	User Agent	Referring URL	Host Name	ISP	More
2020-10-22 00:16:35	103.132.31.43	India, Pune	Mozilla/5.0 (Windows NT 10.0; Win64; x64) AppleWebKit/537.36 (KHTML, like Gecko) Chrome/86.0.4240.80 Safari/537.36 Edg/86.0.622.43	no referrer	103.132.31.43	Ablink Network Opc Private Limited	More Info

As in the image above, we can notice that there is a page claiming to increase Instagram followers. This webpage can be easily used to lure users and attack them and steal their credentials. The person's username and password once entered will be compromised. This is achieved by "Phishing", a process in which the victim is sent a genuinely looking site where the victim's password is immediately lost the moment the victim fills it to login.

```
Username: kknnknk Pass: khjhj Pin:
```

In this way, threat actors can easily hack into personal information and also steal the credentials. Also, these links can be easily manipulated and spoofed in order to make them look legitimate. A common trick that is used by fraudsters is the concept of Homoglyph URLs. This attack has some known aliases: homoglyph attack, script spoofing, and homograph domain name spoofing. Characters—i.e., letters and numbers—that look alike are called homoglyphs or homographs, thus the name of the attack. Examples of such are the Latin small letter O (U+006F) and the Digit zero (U+0030).So, by replacing certain characters in a domain the fraudsters then register the homoglyph domain and use that to lure users.

- www.cybercrimehelpline.in (Homoglyph URL)
- www.cybercrimehelpline.in(Normal URL)

The above two URLs are an example. The first URL is actually a homoglyph URL in which character 'c' & 'i' are replaced with homoglyph characters. The second URL is a legit original URL. An attacker may use the first URL and register that domain and use the link to lure users. One can use the site http://homoglyphs.net/ to send their coded messages in the text files too. Once the file is opened in html, the actual message can be read.

In this way, using various techniques bad actors use links as an important way to not only gather information but also for luring users with an aim to steal the personal and confidential information.

6) IP Details of the Subject

The IP details of any user can be had by couple of ways as explained below:

a) By IMEI: The mobile handset has as many IMEI numbers as the SIM slots. To get the ip details of the user, one can request the police with the IMEI number and they can get the ip details by means of CDR.

b) By IP grabber links: Anyone who sends the links generated either by an online service (generally free) or hosted ip grabber script on any website which would give the IP of the person who clicks it. By logging into www.grabify.link and sending the shortened link to the victim, one can have the following information:

- IPaddress and location city
- Date and time of clicking the link
- Browser used
- Mobile handset and OS
- ISP
- Local IP

On the logged in site, one can view all the details of the subject who has clicked on the link. Similarly, one can find other different sites for getting the current IP of the person.

c) By script hosting: One can host a PHP script on a website and send the link to the victim to get the IP address too. A script can be written in a notepad and extension changed from .txt to .php. The script is as under:

```
<?php
$f=fopen("ip.txt",'a');
$n = time();
$t = gmstrftime("%a, %d %b %Y %H:%M:%S GMT", $n );
fwrite($f,"IP=".$_SERVER["REMOTE_ADDR"]."\n");
fwrite($f,"user agent=".$_SERVER['HTTP_USER_AGENT']."\n");
fwrite($f,"Referer Page=".$_SERVER["HTTP_REFERER"]."\n");
fwrite($f,"TIME=".$t."\n\n\n\n");
fclose($f);
?>
```

The explanation of the script is mentioned below:

For IP Address -

$_SERVER["REMOTE_ADDR"]:

This is used for getting the IP address of the person clicking the link by grabbing the server IP which is connected with the person.

For User Information -

$_SERVER['HTTP_USER_AGENT']:

This provides us the information of the user's information of the operating system and browser.

For Referrer Information -

$_SERVER["HTTP_REFERER"]:

This code is used to get the details of the referrer link.

For Time Information -

$n = time();

$t = gsmtrftime("%a, %d %b %Y %H:%M:%S GMT", $n);

The time of clicking of the URL link by the victim is captured by this.

The script can be hosted on either owned website or on free websites like 000.webhost.com by creating a login. The script of the php can be kept in the folder public_html folder and link shared with the victim. A forwarding line in the script, if required, can also be created in the code to take the subject to a particular existing website to reduce any likely suspicion.

7) QR Codes

The QR codes are very common these days and every payment is easily achieved by scanning the qr code of the merchant. The fraudsters have exploited the technique to hide their malicious links and take away the valuable payments of the victims.

The QR codes can be generated online and can also be decoded online. The url for QR code generation can be searched on the available search engines and similarly, the QR code decoder can also be searched for extracting the information hidden in the QR code.

QR Code Generator:

https://www.the-qrcode-generator.com/

QR Code Decoder:

https://blog.qr4.nl/Online-QR-Code-Decoder.aspx

One can actually insert a phishing link in the QR code as well!!

8) Installing Keyloggers

As per the definition, a keylogger is a computer program that records every keystroke made by a computer user, especially in order to gain fraudulent access to passwords and other confidential information. In simple terms, key logger is software which actually records the keystrokes of the keyboard. Also, there are two types of key loggers – Hardware Keylogger and software keylogger.

Hardware keyloggers are physical devices which once inserted into a computer system, captures all the key strokes and records it. It could be pen drive or an adapter for the keyboard connector.

On the other hand, a software keylogger is a program which once executed runs in the background and captures the keystrokes of the keyboards.

Keyloggers are so efficient that they capture every single key pressed including spaces, special characters, functional keys etc. Today, keyloggers have evolved so rapidly that they're not only sophisticated but also smart. If a keylogger once executed in a system, runs persistently in the system and also sends an email of the keystrokes captures to the attacker. So, after every 15 days or a month or so, all the captured keystrokes from the target system are sent via an email to the attacker.

One of the powerful keylogger is Ardamax Keylogger. There is a free version available but advance and powerful features are only for paid version. https://www.ardamax.com/keylogger/

It has all the features that a complex keylogger must have and is extremely powerful tool.

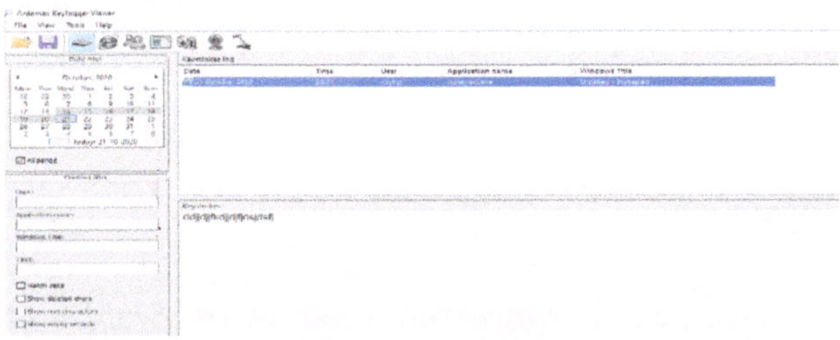

It also includes advance features such as Hidden Mode, Auto Email etc. which makes it one of the best keylogger to purchase. Apart from Ardamax, free keyloggers are also available on GitHub and some of them are uncompiled, of which their entire source code can be modified and a custom keylogger can be made. Similarly, one can find paid keyloggers too available from many vendors.

The preferred keylogger for PC should have the following features for safe monitoring:

a) Stealth

b) Remote Install if available

c) Hidden logs or logs on the cloud

d) FTP (File Transfer Protocol) forwarding features on daily basis

e) AV or defender/FW evasion

One can also have keylogger for mobiles (android and IOS), but for installation, one need to do the following:

a) Go to settings>>search for developers option>>tap continuously for a maximum of 7 times: Notification will show – "You are now a developer"

b) Search "install third party" applications

c) Enable USB debugging if the keylogger is being installed by USB drive

d) Give the required permissions

In case of any difficulty, just go ahead to install and the required pop up will guide you.

9) Password Protection of Word Document and Cracking

Methodology

All word document, excel or powerpoint can be password protected. For protecting the documents, one can select "save as" option and choose to protect besides other ways available for protection.

Cracking the password of the protected document poses practical challenges. To crack passwords of documents, many applications of the protected files and documents exist. The methodology used in cracking the password of the protected files and documents are:

a) Brute force:A brute-force attack consists of an attacker submitting many passwords or passphrases with the hope of eventually guessing a combination correctly. The attacker systematically checks all possible passwords and passphrases until the correct one is found. Alternatively, the attacker can attempt to guess the key which is typically created from the password using a key derivation function. The features contained in the applications for brute force cater for random to pattern based characters comprising of alphabets, numerals, special characters and spaces.

b) Dictionary attack: This type of attack generally caters for dictionary and non dictionary words. A dictionary attack is a method of breaking into a password-protected computer or server by systematically entering every word in a dictionary as a password. A dictionary attack can also be used in an attempt to find the key necessary to decrypt an encrypted message or document. During a dictionary attack, a program systematically enters words from a list as passwords to gain access to a system, account, or encrypted file. A dictionary attack can be performed both online and offline. In an online attack, the attacker repeatedly tries to log in or gain access like any other user. A dictionary for carrying out a dictionary attack can also be created by automatically selecting parameters in applications to get a customized dictionary (usually a text file) to attempt automatically for a successful password.

10) Pc Hardware Essentials-Data Acquisition from Crashed Computers

Every PC System has a certain hardware components like CMOS chip, HDD, processor with motherboard, SMPS, RAM besides display, keyboard, mouse attached for the operation. The basic function of the peripherals and hardware components are as under:-

a) CMOS Chip: CMOS is Complementary Metal Oxide Semiconductor. The CMOS battery powers the BIOS firmware in your laptop. BIOS need to remain operational even when your computer isn't plugged into a power source. The BIOS is the program that starts a computer up, and the CMOS is where the BIOS stores the date, time, and system configuration details it needs to start the computer. CMOS is a type of memory technology, but most people use the term to refer to the chip that stores variable data for start-up. CMOS is an onboard, battery powered semiconductor chip inside computers that stores information. This information ranges from the system time and date to system hardware settings for your computer. When you have forgotten the boot on password, just remove the CMOS battery (No. CR2032) which is on the motherboard and short the jumper earmarked for the purpose or short the nearest IC to discharge the capacitors holding the charge. After this if the system is switched on, the boot on password would not be asked. Alternatively, killcmos.exe also helps in the windows machine to erase the supervisor password. The OS password removal can also be undertaken which will be covered in the HDD section.

b) HDD: A computer hard disk drive (HDD) is a non-volatile memory hardware device that controls the positioning, reading and writing of the hard disk, which furnishes data storage. Hard disk drives are commonly used as the main storage device in a computer. HDDs often store operating system, software programs and other files, and can be found in desktop computers, mobile devices, consumer electronics and enterprise storage arrays in data centers. In a computer, an HDD is commonly found in the drive bay and is connected to the motherboard via an ATA, SATA or SCSI cable. The HDD is also connected to a power supply unit and can keep stored data while powered down.

   Most basic hard drives consist of a number of disk platters that are positioned around a spindle inside a sealed chamber. The chamber also includes read-and-write heads and motors.

   The motor is used to spin the platters, which hold data, at up to 15,000 rotations per minute (a higher RPM number results in faster performance). As the platters spin, a second motor controls the position of the read-and-write heads that magnetically record information to, and read information from, tracks on each platter.

   Unlike hard disks, SSDs contain no moving parts. SSDs also have lower latency than HDDs, and therefore are often favoured to store critical data that needs to be accessed quickly and for applications with a high input/output demand. SSDs are configured to deliver high read and write performance for sequential and random data requests. Additionally, SSDs don't store data magnetically, so the read performance remains steady, regardless of where the data is stored on the drive. If an Operating System is not starting, it could mean that the master boot record on the HDD is corrupted or HDD is not connected properly. Without the OS, it is possible to browse the files in dos mode and recover the HDD contents like documents and files. Alternatively, one can boot by a unix based live cd to crack the OS password.

c) Processor: A processor (CPU) is the logic circuitry that responds to and processes the basic instructions that drive a computer. The CPU is seen as the main and most crucial integrated circuitry (IC) chip in a computer, as it is responsible for interpreting most of computers commands. A CPU interprets the program's instructions and creates the output that you interface with when you're using a computer. A processor is made up of hardware that works together to deliver information, allowing your computer to complete the tasks that you request when you open an application or make changes to a file.

d) Motherboard: A Motherboard is the spine of your PC, it is the link between all the different components inside your computer. One of the major functions of a motherboard is to act as the "hub" to which other computer devices connect. A board can come in many formations to fit different needs, budgets and speeds. The motherboard accommodates the central processing unit (CPU), RAM, expansion slots, heat sink/fan assembly, BIOS chip, chip set, and the embedded wires that interconnect the motherboard components. Sockets, internal and external connectors, and various ports are also placed on the motherboard.

e) SMPS: SMPS is the abbreviation of switching mode power supply, a kind of high-frequency power conversion device and a power supply device. Its function is to convert a level of voltage to the voltage or current required by the client through different forms of architecture. It is a PSU (power supply unit) and is usually used in computers to change the voltage to the appropriate range for the computer. An SMPS adjusts output voltage and current between different electrical configurations by switching the basics of typically lossless storage such as capacitors and inductors. PC SMPS provide +3.3V, +5V, and +12V at high ampere (A) ratings as well as some low current negative voltages (blended with plentiful over voltage and short circuit protection).

Symptoms of a failing computer power supply are :

- Random computer crashes.
- Random blue screen crashes.
- Extra noise coming from the PC case.
- Recurring failure of PC components.
- PC won't start but your case fans spin.

f) RAM: It is a vital part of every computer system, random access memory (RAM) provides short term storage space for data and program code. Random access memory, RAM, provides short term storage space for data and program code that a computer processor is in the act of using, or which it expects to use imminently. Higher the RAM, faster would be the system.

g) Display: To display the working and output of any program. The display function provides information about the kind of values that are the result of executing a statement or expression. This information is useful for understanding how a program or script works.

h) Keyboard/Mouse: These are input devices for performing operations on a computer system. The input of these peripherals can also be interpreted by means of keyloggers (hardware and software)

11) Cracking PC and File Passwords

A Computer System has two types of passwords: Boot-on password and Operating System password (OS) password. The boot-on password appears before the OS is loaded on the system. The OS password is for the user or default account holder. In earlier windows OS, the password used to be any numeric, alphanumeric or words/phrase, but in windows system if the user has put the login id as his/her email id, the password for the same can still be cracked. Following are some of the methods to crack the locked PC passwords:

a) The boot on password can be bypassed after disabling it from the super user mode. One can login to the administrator mode or supervisor mode at the time of the booting up process by clicking on certain key sets. The complete list of such keys can be found for all types of laptops by searching on the internet.

b) The OS password can be cracked by Konboot application. One needs to boot up the system with a konboot disc/pen drive and crack the password. Similarly, L0hp is also considered an option to get the OS and administrator's password.

c) The supervisor/administrator password which is saved on the CMOS can be killed by a simple application killcmos.exe available for free.

12) Cyber Forensics and Anti Forensics Methodology

The methodologies for undertaking Cyber Forensics and Anti Forensics are explained below:

Cyber Forensics

Cyber forensics (also known as computer forensic science) is a branch of digital forensic science pertaining to evidence found in computers and digital storage media. Evidence from computer forensics investigations is usually subjected to the same guidelines and practices of other digital evidence. It generally involves extraction of digital evidences, preservation and analysis for legal or non legal purposes.

Important Forensics Tools

Cyber Forensics tools are primarily used to establish the evidences of the investigations where the user has committed any misappropriation of any data whether financial or non financial against any person or company. This would involve extraction of lost or available evidence for any likely future judicial trial.

The cyber forensics tools are available for conducting investigation for windows, linux, MAC and or mobile devices on IOS or android. The most used tools are enlisted below:

Computer Forensics Tool List (Published on Wikipedia and updated by CCH)

Name	Platform	License	Version	Description
Autopsy	Windows, macOS, Linux	GPL	4.16	A digital forensics platform and GUI to The Sleuth Kit
Belkasoft X	Windows	proprietary	1.0.6233	Digital forensic suite by Belkasoft, which supports computer and mobile forensics in a single tool
COFEE	Windows	proprietary	n/a	A suite of tools for Windows developed by Microsoft
Digital Forensics Framework	Unix-like/Windows	GPL	1.3	Framework and user interfaces dedicated to digital forensics
Elcomsoft Premium Forensic Bundle	Windows, macOS	proprietary	1435	Set of tools for encrypted systems & data decryption and password recovery

Name	Platform	License	Version	Description
E3: Universal Software	Windows, macOS, Linux	GPL	2.6	E3:Universal develop by Paraben Corporation is and end-to-end DFIR solution that can work through ALL types of digital data: computers, email, internet data, smartphones, &IoT devices.
EnCase	Windows	proprietary	8.11	Digital forensics suite created by Guidance Software
Forensic Explorer	Windows	proprietary	5.4.2.1122	Digital forensics suite created by GetData
FTK	Windows	proprietary	7.3	Multi-purpose tool, FTK is a court-cited digital investigations platform built for speed, stability and ease of use.
IPED[4]	Unix-like/Windows	GPL	3.17.2	Digital forensics tool created by the Brazilian Federal Police
ISEEK[5]	Windows	proprietary	1	Hybrid-forensics tool running only in memory - designed for large networked environments
IsoBuster	Windows	proprietary	4.7	Essential light weight tool to inspect any type data carrier, supporting a wide range of file

Name	Platform	License	Version	Description
				systems, with advanced export functionality.
Mobile Device Investigator	Windows,	proprietary	2.1	iOS and Android digital forensics and smartphone triage tool by ADF_Solutions
Netherlands Forensic Institute / Xiraf[6] / HANSKEN[7]	n/a	proprietary	n/a	Computer-forensic online service.
Open Computer Forensics Architecture	Linux	LGPL/GPL	2.3.0	Computer forensics framework for CF-Lab environment
OSForensics[8][9]	Windows	proprietary	8	Multi-purpose forensic tool
PTK Forensics	LAMP	proprietary	2.0	GUI for The Sleuth Kit
SANS Investigative Forensics Toolkit - SIFT	Ubuntu		2.1	Multi-purpose forensic operating system
SPEKTOR Forensic Intelligence[10]	Unix-like	proprietary	6.x	Easy to use, comprehensive forensic tool used worldwide by LE/Military/Agencies/ Corporates - includes rapid imaging and fully

Name	Platform	License	Version	Description
				automated analysis.
The Coroner's Toolkit	Unix-like	IBM Public License	1.19	A suite of programs for Unix analysis
The Sleuth Kit	Unix-like/Windows	IPL, CPL, GPL	4.1.2	A library of tools for both Unix and Windows
Windows To Go	n/a	proprietary	n/a	Bootable operating system
X-Ways Forensics	Windows	proprietary	n/a	Supports images and a bunch of volumes. And also memory and ram analysis

Memory forensics

Memory forensics tools are used to acquire or analyze a computer's volatile memory (RAM). They are often used in incident response situations to preserve evidence in memory that would be lost when a system is shut down, and to quickly detect stealthy malware by directly examining the operating system and other running software in memory.

Name	Vendor or sponsor	Platform	License
Belkasoft Live RAM Capturer	Belkasoft	Windows	free
Volatility	Volatile Systems	Windows and Linux	free (GPL)
WindowsSCOPE	BlueRISC	Windows	proprietary

Mobile device forensics

Mobile forensics tools tend to consist of both a hardware and software component. Mobile phones come with a diverse range of connectors, the hardware devices support a number of different cables and perform the same role as a write blocker in computer devices.

Name	Platform	License	Version	Description
MicroSystemation XRY/XACT[11]	Windows	Proprietary		Hardware/software package, specializes in deleted data
Celbrite				
MOBILedit				
IFK				

Software forensics

Software forensics is the science of analyzing software source code or binary code to determine whether intellectual property infringement or theft occurred. It is the center piece of lawsuits, trials, and settlements when companies are in dispute over issues involving software patents, copyrights, and trade secrets. Software forensics tools can compare code to determine correlation, a measure that can be used to guide a software forensics expert.

Other

Name	Platform	License	Version	Description
Snap PC Forensics Tool	Windows	CCH	1.2	For live window based digital forensics

Name	Platform	License	Version	Description
Snap Linux Forensics Tool	Linux	CCH	1.0	For live Linux machine forensics
TOR & VPN Forensics	Windows	CCH	1.0	For establishing traces and evidences of a suspected windows machine

Anti-Forensics

Anti-forensics tactics are used by cybercriminals to disrupt evidence gathering and analysis processes. The primary purpose of anti-forensic techniques is to make it hard or even impossible for a cyber forensic investigator to conduct a digital investigation. The methods used for anti forensics focuses on changing the meta data of a file, changing the log files with spurious data, shredding the files beyond recovery possibility. The manipulation of the log details can be changed by the extraction of the files, changing or corrupting the data and positioning it back to its original place. Many logs can be changed through the registry files. Some of the anti forensics tools are as under:

a) bc wipe: BCWipe can run from either My Computer or from a command line prompt. It has a powerful set of utilities. One can create customized wiping of data of a windows or MAC computer system.

Web link: https://www.jetico.com/data-wiping/wipe-files-bcwipe

b) srm: The tool is used by the fraudsters to overwrite the data in the largest files before unlinking them. It prevents command line recovery of the data by examining the raw block device. It is a linux based tool

Web link:

http://srm.sourceforge.net/&http://srm.sourceforge.net/srm.html

c) wipe: Ya-wipe is a tool that efficiently does the degaussing of the surface of a hard disk, to make the retrieval the data impossible. It helps deletion of the data from the magnetic media. It is a Linux based tool.

Web link: http://wipe.sourceforge.net/

d) DBAN: The name Darik's Boot and Nuke (DBAN) is a tool which is installed on a drive to boot up and securely wipe the dard disks of most computers. It completely deletes the contents of any hard disk it detects and makes it difficult for forensically extracting the deleted data from windows OS

Web link: https://dban.org/

e) Diskzapper: It is a tool which starts erasing the disks automatically after the booting process. It does not use the keyboard and monitor without any user interference. The tool is a linux based.

Web link: Not available. But it can be downloaded from internet as it is freely available through search engines.

f) SecureIT: This is an encrypting tool with full features for files and folders. It is based on 448-bit encryption with blowfish algorithm. Has file shredder and can generate self decrypting email attachments. Made for windows 32 bit and 64 bit.

Web link:

https://www.cypherix.com/secureit2000/index.htm

g) CryptoMite: This is also used by hackers to encrypt, decrypt and wipe the files and folders of any type. Supports various encryption engines and zip compression utility. It also supports self-extracting encrypted ZIP files and email facility. This was made for upto windows7. One can try if it works for higher version of windows.

Web link: http://www.baxbex.com/cryptomite.html

h) Evidence Eliminator: This tool completely destroys the windows SWAP file, application logs, temp files, recycle bin, registry backup files, clipboard data, start menu recent documents, history, etc.
Web link: https://evidence-eliminator.en.softonic.com/

i) Tracks Eraser Pro: This tool clears all the tracks of the internet activities of the computer system. The cache, cookies, history, browser history and other internet details can be erased from the browser related internet information in a single click.

Web link: http://www.acesoft.net/

j) Declasfy: This tool wipes the hard disks and storage media. It writes the entire disk with hex0s, then 1s(0xff). It is used to change the dates and manipulate the events log to confuse the investigator.

Web link: https://ccm.net/download/download-15746-evidence-eliminator and https://evidence-eliminator.en.softonic.com/

k) Invisible Secrets: This tool encrypts your data and files for safe keeping or for secure transfer on the net. It hides the data like audio files, image files and web pages from the investigator too.

Web link: https://www.east-tec.com/invisiblesecrets/

l) BatchPurifier: It is a tool to remove more than 60 types of hidden data from 25 file types in addition to the Msoffice documents. It is made to hide data stored in these file types that may contain confidential & private information. It can remove hidden data even from the compressed zip files.

Web link:

http://www.digitalconfidence.com/BatchPurifier.html

m) Mantra: This application is a collection of free and open source tools integrated in a web browser which is considered handy for students, penetration testers, web application developers and security professionals.

Web link: https://getmantra.com/web-app-security-testing-with-browsers/

n) Attention-Deficit-Disorder (ADD): This tool is used for polluting the physical memory with fake artifacts to achieve anti-analysis objective. It's an open source tool and works with windows7 OS.

Web link: https://code.google.com/archive/p/attention-deficit-disorder/

o) Data Wiping Software: DBAN is a free erasure software for home user. It deletes the contents of any hard disk that it can detect. This tool us useful to remove the data of a computer system before giving it out for recycling.

Web link: https://dban.org/

p) Blancco5 and Blancoo Flash: The Blancco5 data erasure tool erases the data from the storage media of a computer system or server. The Blancco Flash ensures data erasure before one considers disposing of the storage devices, USB drives or memory cards, etc.

Web link: https://www.blancco.com/products/removable-media-eraser/

r) Ontrack Eraser Degausser: This tool is used to destroy the complete data in seconds as claimed. It offers to delete large volume of data of an organization from multiple computer systems by hardware means.

Web link: https://www.blancco.com/products/data-erasure-hardware/

s) Blancco Mobile: This tool is designed to securely erase the smartphone's internal and external memory data as factory setting of a smartphone only resets the mobile applications and functioning without erasing the old data which is inherently available in the internal memory in a hidden form.

Web link: https://www.blancco.com/solutions/mobile-processors/

t) Bitraser: This tool is a certified and secure data erasing software which permanently deletes hard disk data beyond the scope of data recovery. It supports multiple international erasure standards.

Web link: https://bitraser.com/

u) Other Miscellaneous tools: There are many other tools which pose challenge in any forensics investigation. The list of such tools are described below:

For Windows OS:-

i) BrowseList:-BrowseList retrieves the browse list in a Windows network. The output list contains computer names and the roles they play in the network. For example, you can see which PDC, BDC, stand-alone servers and workstations. You can also see the system comments (which can be fascinating reading).

Usage instructions:-Download the exe file and run it from the Command Prompt. If you run it without parameters, it asks your system for the browse list. If you specify an IP address as the parameter, it asks that system for the browse list instead. One can redirect the output to a file by appending for example "> file.txt" at the end of what you write at the Command Prompt. You can stop the output by appending "| more". One can write to retrieve the browse list from a remote system like "browselist 192.168.1.1". One must run the file from a Command Prompt to avoid popping up of different window while double clicking.

Download link:

https://vidstromlabs.com/freetools/browselist/

ii) CPUID:-CPUID shows detailed information about various capabilities and properties of your CPU.

Usage instructions:-Download the file and run it from a Command Prompt.

Download link: https://vidstromlabs.com/freetools/cpuid/

iii) CrashProcess:-Pass CrashProcess a PID, and it crashes the process if you have sufficient permissions. It can be useful for testing stuff.

Usage instructions:-Download the file and run it from a Command Prompt with the PID passed as an argument.

Download link:

https://vidstromlabs.com/freetools/crashprocess/

iv)DBProbe:-DBProbe checks the directed broadcast ping amplification factor for a network.

Usage instructions:-Download the exe file and run it from the Command Prompt. It will give you the instructions you need. One must run the file from a Command Prompt to avoid popping up of different window while double clicking. To configure Cisco router to block directed broadcast pings IOS 12.0 and higher blocks them by default. Otherwise you have to change the configuration for each interface to "no IP directed-broadcast."

Download link:

https://vidstromlabs.com/freetools/dbprobe/

v) DumpUsers:-DumpUsers can dump account names and information even though “RestrictAnonymous” has been set to 1.

Usage instructions:Download the exe file and run it from the Command Prompt. It will give you the instructions you need."-type" parameter must be "dc" if the target is a Domain Controller, and "notdc" if it isn't. Relative ID (RID) is the last part of a Security Identifier (SID). DumpUsers will list all accounts with RID's between the start and stop values. "-mode" parameter can be either "quiet" - list only account names - or "verbose" - list information about each account too. Set RestrictAnonymous to 2.

Download link:

https://vidstromlabs.com/freetools/dumpusers/

vi) EFS View:-EFSView lists the users who have ordinary decryption keys or recovery keys for an EFS encrypted file.

Usage instructions:-Download the exe file and run it from the Command Prompt. It will give you the instructions you need. One must run the file from a Command Prompt to avoid popping up of different window while double clicking.

Download link:

https://vidstromlabs.com/freetools/efsview/

vii) EtherChange:-EtherChange can change the Ethernet address of the network adapters in Windows.

Usage instructions:-Download the exe file and run it from a Command Prompt. It will give you the instructions you need. EtherChange only works if your account is in the Administrators group. One must run the file from a Command Prompt to avoid popping up of different window while double clicking.

Download link:

https://vidstromlabs.com/freetools/etherchange/

viii) ExploreLibs:-ExploreLibs is a tool for viewing the contents of LIB files.

Usage instructions:-Download the file and run it. It is pretty self-explanatory.

Download link:

https://vidstromlabs.com/freetools/explorelibs/

ix) FindIDT:-FindIDT searches for and prints the IDTs in a physical memory dump.

Usage instructions: Download the exe file and run it from a Command Prompt. It will give you the instructions you need. One must run the file from a Command Prompt to avoid popping up of different window while double clicking.

Download link:

https://vidstromlabs.com/freetools/findidt/

x)GPList:-GPList lists information about the applied Group Policies.

Usage instructions: Download the exe file and run it from a Command Prompt. It will give you the instructions you need. One must run the file from a Command Prompt to avoid popping up of different window while double clicking. One can redirect the output to a file by appending for example "> file.txt" at the end of what you write at the Command Prompt. You can stop the output by appending "| more". GPO are listed in the order they are applied. The one that is applied first comes first, and so on.

Download link: https://vidstromlabs.com/freetools/gplist/

xi) GSD:-GSD (Get Service DACL) gives you the DACL (Discretionary Access Control List) of any service you specify as a command line option.

Usage instructions:-Download the exe file and run it from the Command Prompt. It will give you the instructions you need. The service name to give as a parameter is the same name as you can see in the services applet in the control panel. GSD only works if your account is in the Administrators group. One can redirect the output to a file by appending for example "> file.txt" at the end of what you write at the Command Prompt. You can stop the output by appending "| more". All services have corresponding DACL's which control access to them - services are securable objects in Windows NT. This isn't the same thing as the permissions set on the services registry keys, but instead, permissions set on the services as objects. One must run the file from a Command Prompt to avoid popping up of different window while double clicking.

Download link: https://vidstromlabs.com/freetools/gsd/

xii) Inzider:-Inzider shows which processes listen at which ports. Inzider was the first tool that could do that in Windows, back in the 1990s. This updated version shows more information than before, including IPv6 information, svchost.exe service information, and the date and time each port was opened. Also, it doesn't have any of the stability problems that the old versions had.

Usage instructions:-Download the exe file and run it from the Command Prompt. Inzider gives the most information if you run the Command Prompt as administrator. One can redirect the output to a file by appending for example "> file.txt" at the end of what you write at the Command Prompt. You can stop the output by appending "| more". One must run the file from a Command Prompt to avoid popping up of different window while double clicking. Here, IP address "0.0.0.0" means that the process has bound the port at all available IP addresses.

Download link:

https://vidstromlabs.com/freetools/inzider/

xiii) IPSecScan:-IPSecScan is a tool that can scan either a single IP address or a range of IP addresses looking for systems that are IPSec enabled. It was the first IPSec scanner out there.

Usage instructions:-Download the exe file and run it from the Command Prompt. One must run the file from a Command Prompt to avoid popping up of different window while double clicking. Here, Enabled means that the system has IPSec enabled. Disabled means that it either doesn't support IPSec, has IPSec disabled, or that it is configured not to reveal to you that it has IPSec enabled. Indeterminable means that the scanner isn't sure if IPSec is enabled or disabled, it is also the label put on IP addresses which are not in use at all. If the scanner tells you that a system is IPSec enabled you can trust the result almost completely. The scanner isn't capable of telling you for sure that a system does not have IPSec enabled, simply because of the way the technology works, so the result Disabled is a qualified guess. If you receive the result Indeterminable and you know that the IP address is in use, there is a high probability that the system has IPSec enabled, but the scanner isn't completely sure.

Download link:

https://vidstromlabs.com/freetools/ipsecscan/

xiv) ListDrivers:-ListDrivers lists the loaded kernel drivers.

Usage instructions

Download the exe file and run it from the Command Prompt. One must run the file from a Command Prompt to avoid popping up of different window while double clicking.

Download link:

https://vidstromlabs.com/freetools/listdrivers

xv) ListModules:-ListModules lists the modules (EXEs and DLLs) that are loaded into a process.

Usage instructions:-Download the exe file and run it from the Command Prompt. One must run the file from a Command Prompt to avoid popping up of different window while double clicking. It has got two versions of i.e of 32 bit version and 64 bit version.

Download link:

https://vidstromlabs.com/freetools/listmodules/

xvi) ListObj:-ListObj prints the entire Windows object space.

Usage instructions:-Download the exe file and run it from the Command Prompt. One must run the file from a Command Prompt to avoid popping up of different window while double clicking.

Download link:

https://vidstromlabs.com/freetools/listobj/

xvii) LNS – List NTFS Streams:-LNS is a tool that searches for NTFS streams (aka alternate data streams or multiple data streams).

Usage instructions:-Download the exe file and run it from the Command Prompt. Run the Command Prompt as administrator. One must run the file from a Command Prompt to avoid popping up of different window while double clicking. One can redirect the output to a file by appending for example "> file.txt" at the end of what you write at the Command Prompt. You can stop the output by appending "| more".

Download link: https://vidstromlabs.com/freetools/lns/

xviii) MACMatch:-MACMatch lets you search for files by their last write, last access or creation time without changing any of these times.

Usage instructions:-Download the exe file and run it from the Command Prompt. Run the Command Prompt as administrator. One must run the file from a Command Prompt to avoid popping up of different window while double clicking. One can redirect the output to a file by appending for example "> file.txt" at the end of what you write at the Command Prompt. You can stop the output by appending "| more".

Download link:

https://vidstromlabs.com/freetools/macmatch

xix) NSCopy:-NSCopy works as a copy command with one big difference from others. If you have the "Back up files and directories" user right, you can copy files even if you don't have any explicit permission to read them. It doesn't take ownership of the file to do it.

Usage instructions:-Download the exe file and run it from the Command Prompt. One must run the file from a Command Prompt to avoid popping up of different window while double clicking. By default, the Administrators group and the Backup Operators group, but an administrator can give it to any account. The difference is that an administrator can copy the file without taking the extra steps of taking ownership and then giving it back (using for example SetOwner).

It is a common misunderstanding that whenever an administrator doesn't have permission to read a file, he/she has to take ownership of the file and then give himself/herself permission to read it. Afterwards, the administrator wouldn't be able to give back the ownership since you can never give but only take ownership (which is also a misunderstanding, see SetOwner). However, NSCopy demonstrates that this is a misunderstanding and that there is no need at all to take ownership, as generally misunderstood, see SetOwner). However, NSCopy demonstrates that this is a misunderstanding and that there is no need at all to take ownership.

Download link:

https://vidstromlabs.com/freetools/nscopy/

xx) Periscope:-Periscope is a PE file inspection tool. It works on ordinary 32-bit files as well as 64-bitand .NET ones.

Usage instructions:-Download the exe file and run it from the Command Prompt. It will give you the instructions you need. One must run the file from a Command Prompt to avoid popping up of different window while double clicking. One can redirect the output to a file by appending for example "> file.txt" at the end of what you write at the Command Prompt. You can stop the output by appending "| more". To get a warning that the entry point does not point into the code segment means that when you run the file, the first instruction that is executed isn't located at any of the places where instructions are typically located. This can be a sign of virus infection. Please note that even if you don't get this warning, the file can still be infected by a virus!

We cannot trust that all DLL's and functions in them that the file uses are listed in the imports table. The only way to be entirely sure of what a file does is to disassemble it and go through every single instruction. The function ordinals are the numbers before the function names in the import table. The function ordinals and the RVA's in that order are the numbers before the function names in the export table. One where the hash value is rotated 13 positions to the right for each character and then has the character value added to it.

Download link:

https://vidstromlabs.com/freetools/periscope/

xxi) PMDump:-PMDump is a tool that lets you dump the memory contents of a process to a file without stopping the process.

Usage instructions:-Download the exe file and run it from the Command Prompt. One must run the file from a Command Prompt to avoid popping up of different window while double clicking.

Download link:

https://vidstromlabs.com/freetools/pmdump/

xxii) PromiscDetect:-PromiscDetect checks locally if your network adapter(s) is running in promiscuous mode, which may be a sign that you have a sniffer running on your computer. It was the first tool that could do that in Windows.

Usage instructions:-Download the exe file and run it from the Command Prompt. One must run the file from a Command Prompt to avoid popping up of different window while double clicking. Directed,

Multicast and Broadcast would be the response for an adapter in "normal" mode. It's reliable as long as the attacker doesn't intercept and modify things somewhere between the tool and the adapter. Look at it this way: if the tool tells you that the adapter is in promiscuous mode it probably is - but if it doesn't you shouldn't just assume that the adapter isn't in promiscuous mode. VMWare puts your adapter in promiscuous mode even if you're not running a sniffer.

Download link:

https://vidstromlabs.com/downloads/promiscdetect.exe

xxiii) SetOwner:-SetOwner allows you to set file ownership to any account, as long as you have the "Restore files and directories" user right.

Usage instructions:-Download the exe file and run it from the Command Prompt. It will give you the instructions you need. It is possible to set file ownership to any account but you need the "Restore files and directories" user right. The "Take ownership of files and other objects" user right is the one administrators typically use to take ownership, but it only allows you to set ownership to your own account. By default, the Administrators group and the Backup Operators group, but an administrator can give it to any account. One must run the file from a Command Prompt to avoid popping up of different window while double clicking.

Download link:

https://vidstromlabs.com/freetools/setowner/

xxiv) SIMQuery:-SIMQuery is a tool that retrieves the ICCID and IMSI from a GSM SIM card.

Usage instructions:-Download the exe file and run it from the Command Prompt. One must run the file froma Command Prompt to avoid popping up of different window while double clicking. Youneed a smart card reader that is compatible with the Windows smart card subsystem,and you probably also need an ID-1 to Plug-in adapter card.

Download link:

https://vidstromlabs.com/freetools/simquery/

xxv) UndeleteSMS:-UndeleteSMS can recover deleted SMS messages from a GSM SIM card.

Usage instructions:-Download the exe file and run it from the Command Prompt. You need a smart card reader that is compatible with the Windows smart card subsystem. You probably also need a Plug-in (GSM SIM card size) to ID-1 (regular smart card size) adapter card, so the SIM card fits into the reader physically. A reader called ChipDrive Micro RS232 from Towitoko can be used. Dedicated GSM SIM card readers are usually not compatible with the Windows smart card subsystem. They are printed in the Command Prompt window. "Message is not in default alphabet [40] cannot decode" means that the entry is an EMS or MMS instead of an ordinary SMS. One must run the file from a Command Prompt to avoid popping up of different window while double clicking.

Download link:

https://vidstromlabs.com/freetools/undeletesms/

xxvi) Winfo:-Winfo uses null sessions to remotely try to retrieve lists of, and information about, useraccounts, workstation/interdomain/server trust accounts, shares (also hidden), sessions, logged in users, and password/lockout policy. It also identifies the built-in Administrator and Guest accounts, even if their names have been changed.

Usage instructions:-Download the exe file and run it from the Command Prompt. One must run the file from a Command Prompt to avoid popping up of different window while double clicking. One can redirect the output to a file by appending for example "> file.txt" at the end of what you write at the Command Prompt. You can stop the output by appending "| more".

Download link: https://vidstromlabs.com/freetools/winfo/

xxvii) WKML:-WKML (Windows Kernel Module Loader) is a tool for loading and unloading kernel modules in Windows. It can also display a list of the currently loaded modules.

Usage instructions:-Download the file and run it. It should be pretty self-explanatory for someone who develops kernel modules.

Download like: https://vidstromlabs.com/freetools/wkml/

xxviii) WPSweep:-WPSweep is a simple ping sweeper, that is, it pings a range of IP addresses and liststhe ones that reply.

Usage instructions:-Download the exe file and run it from the Command Prompt. One must run the file froma Command Prompt to avoid popping up of different window while double clicking.

Download link:

https://vidstromlabs.com/freetools/wpsweep/

xxix) FreeDOS Tool:-TAFT (The ATA Forensics Tool) is an ATA (IDE) forensics tool that communicates directly with the ATA controller. It can retrieve various information about a hard disk, as well as look at and change the HPA and DCO settings. One must boot from a FreeDOS floppy or USB storage device and run TAFT from there. TAFT isn't a Windows program since it needs free access to the ATA hard disk controller.

Usage instructions:-Download the exe file and copy it to a FreeDOS boot floppy. Boot from the floppy and run the tool. One must boot from a FreeDOS floppy and run TAFT from there. TAFT isn't a Windows program since it needs free access to the ATA hard disk controller.

Download link:https://vidstromlabs.com/freetools/taft/

13) Steganography and Encryption

The word "Steganography" in Greek means 'hidden writing'. It is a method of hiding secret data, by embedding it into an audio, video, image or text file. It is one of the methods employed to protect secret or sensitive data from the prying eyes. Some of the favoured steganography tools are explained below.

a) Steghide

Steghide is open-source steganography software that lets you hide your secret file in an image or audio file. You will not notice any change in the image or audio file. However, your secret file will be inside the original image or audio file.

This is command-line software. Therefore, you need to learn the commands to use the tool. Commands will be used to embed files in the image or audio file. In addition, to extract your file from the image or audio file, you need to use another command.

Steghide is one of the cross-platform steganography software that has been developed by Stefan Hetzl. The tool can be used to hide various kind of data in images and audio files.

Download link:

https://www.softpedia.com/get/Security/Encrypting/SteganPEG.shtml

c) Xiao Steganography

Xiao Steganography is free software that can be used to hide secret files in BMP images or WAV files. Using the tool is easy: you can just open the software and load any BMP image or WAV file to its interface. Then add a file you want to hide.

It also supports encryption. You can select from various algorithms like RC4, Triple DES, DES, Triple DES 112, RC2 and hashing SHA, MD4, MD2 and MD5. Select any one from the list and then save the target file.

To read the hidden message from this file, you will have to use this software again. This software will read the file and will decode the hidden file from it. You cannot extract the hidden file with any other software.

CNET is known for offering installation of third-party browser extensions. Be sure to see what other software and adware this tool is offering along with the installation of Xiao Steganography.

Download link

:https://download.cnet.com/Xiao-Steganography/3000-2092_4-10541494.html

d) Image Steganography

Image Steganography is another free program for hiding your information in image files. You can hide text messages or files inside an image file. Just select the source file in which you want to hide the secret message and then select the file to hide or write the text message to hide. Select the output image location and then click on the start button to start encoding the file.

The encoded image will have the secret message inside the image. You can use the decode option of the same tool to decode the hidden file or message.

Download link:
https://archive.codeplex.com/?p=imagesteganography

e) Crypture

Crypture is another command-line tool that performs steganography. You can use this tool to hide your sensitive data inside a BMP image file. But there is one requirement: the BMP file should be eight times larger than the data file you want to hide inside the BMP file. If you have a small amount of data to hide, you can use this tool.

This tool is very small and is only 6KB in size. It does not need any kind of installation.

Download link:
http://sourceforge.net/projects/crypture/

f) SteganographX Plus

SteganographX Plus is another small tool that lets you hide your confidential data inside a BMP image. It also does not need any installation and is of only 496 KB in size.

This is simple and offers an easy-to use-interface. You can use this tool to hide your sensitive data inside a BMP file and recover your data from that file.

Download link:
https://www.bestfreewaredownload.com/freeware/t-free-steganographx-plus-freeware-yeipgmrk.html

g) rSteg

rSteg is a Java-based tool that lets you hide textual data inside an image. It has two buttons: one to encrypt and second to decrypt the text. Just select the image file, enter the PIN and then enter the text which you want to hide in the image. It will generate a target image file with the hidden text inside. If you want to read that text again, use this tool and select the decrypt option.

Download link:

http://www.softpedia.com/get/Security/Security-Related/rSteg.shtml

h) SuitePicsel

SSuitePicsel is a free portable application to hide text inside an image file. However, it has a different approach. It uses the image file as a key to protect your hidden text inside an image.

Don't be confused. Actually, this tool can hide text inside an image file. Nevertheless, to hide and reveal text inside an image, you need to enter another image as a key. To hide text inside the image, select the image in which you want to hide the text and select another image for the key. Now you can hide your text inside the first image. To reveal the text, you need to enter the key image.

Download link:
http://www.ssuitesoft.com/ssuitepicselsecurity.htm

i) Our Secret

Our Secret is another tool that is used to hide sensitive information in a file. The interface of the tool is divided into two parts: one part is to hide the data in a file and the other part is to reveal.

You need to select the carrier file in which you want to hide your data. Then select the data or file you want to hide. Enter the password to encrypt your message and then hide the data in the file. Use the same tool again to reveal the data.
Download link:
http://steganography.findmysoft.com/

j) Camouflage

Camouflage is another steganography tool that lets you hide any type of file inside of a file. There is no kind of restriction in the software for hiding the file.

Use of the tool is simple and easy: you can just right-click on any file and select the Camouflage option. To extract your sensitive data from the file, right-click and select Uncamouflage. You can also set a password to encrypt the hidden data inside the file.

The project is no longer in development, but you can use the old file for your work. It still performs well and you can use it to hide your confidential data inside an image.

Download link:

http://camouflage.unfiction.com/Download.html

k) OpenStego

If you are searching for a steganography tool, OpenStego is another good option. You can attach any kind of secret message file in an image file. You can hide images in BMP, GIF, JPEG, JPG, PNG and WBMP.

You can hide data in these files and take output as a PNG file. The same software will be used to reveal data from the output file. It also uses a password to encrypt your data along with hiding inside the image file. This tool is open-source and developed in Java.

Download link:

http://sourceforge.net/projects/openstego/files/

l) SteganPEG

SteganPEG lets you hide any kind of file in a JPG image file. You can attach any file and give a password to hide inside a JPG file. Only SteganPEG can extract your file from that output JPG image. The output file will act like an ordinary image file and one cannot tell that the image was modified just by looking at it.

The interface of the software is simple with fewer options. One can easily use this tool to hide data in a JPG image file.

Download link:

https://www.softpedia.com/get/Security/Encrypting/SteganPEG.shtml

m) Hide'N'Send

Hide'N'Send is a small utility which offers steganography. It lets you hide any kind of file behind a JPG image file. It supports hashing and encryption too. This means that you can hide your data by encrypting. This adds an extra layer of security.

The interface of the tool is simple and offers two tabs — one to hide data and other to extract data. You can select the options accordingly. Just run the tool, select the image file, then select the file which you want to hide, select the encryption type and then hide the data in the image. Use the same tool again to extract the hidden information in the image.

Steganography is an effective way of secure communication. You can first encrypt a confidential file and then hide it inside an image of another kind of file before sending it to some other. It will decrease the chances of being intercepted.

If you just send the file by encrypting it, the attacker will try to decrypt it by various ways. However, if he only finds a normal image file, he'll have no clue.

Download link:http://download.cnet.com/Hide-N-Send/3000-2092_4-75728348.html

14) Detection of steganography

The detection of steganography is important for any forensics examination. The available tools are checked if installed on the computer system. The investigator will need to be updated on the type of tools and recovery methods. Some of the tools available are enlisted in the following paragraphs.Other Stego tools are:

StegoHunt™MP

- Quickly identify if steganography is present in your investigations by scanning for thousands of steganography, stegware and data hiding applications using advanced, fast search methods
- Identify suspect carrier files that otherwise go undetected, including program artifacts, program signatures, and statistical anomalies
- Generate case-specific reports for management or court presentation
- Utilize multiple operational discovery modes, including directory, drive, archives, drive image, and network path

StegoAnalyst™

- Steganography analysis tool that provides deep investigation of detected images and audio files
- Utilize the file viewing panel to display the individual file attributes, including image details, discrete cosine transform (DCT) coefficients, and color pairs
- Select from various filter options for further presentation and analysis, such as least significant bit (LSB) of specific colors.

StegoBreak™

- Quickly and easily crack and extract payloads from many carrier files using a simple point and click interface
- Leverage the popular password dictionaries included in order to execute a dictionary attack

- Easily bring in other dictionaries, as well as create your own, to expand your dictionary attack

How is it different from cryptography?

Cryptography makes the data unreadable, or hides the meaning of the data by encrypting it, while steganography hides the very existence of the data.

16. Cryptography Tools and Techniques

Cryptography can be defined as the process of concealing the contents of a message from all except those who know the key. Cryptography can be used for many purposes, but there are two types of cryptographic algorithms you need to understand, symmetric and asymmetric.

There are two main types of cryptography systems: symmetric ("private key") and asymmetric ("public key"). Symmetric key system requires both the sender and the recipient to have the same key unlike the asymmetric keys.

Cryptanalysis

Cryptology is divided into – Cryptography and Cryptanalysis.

Cryptography deals with the creation of ciphers and cryptosystems. Cryptanalysis deals with the breaking of ciphers and cryptosystems.

Cryptanalysis can be done by various approaches or attacks like brute force, chosen plaintext and man in the middle attack. Web-based cryptanalysis tools are also available that can break the cryptosystems, teach about network security and test the cryptosystems in general.

Dictionary attack

A dictionary attack is a method of breaking into a password-protected computer or server by systematically entering every word in a dictionary as a password. A dictionary attack can also be used in an attempt to find the key necessary to decrypt an encrypted message or document.

Brute force attack

This is an old methodology to try a combination of the selected input types of characters. It utilizes every possibility until a match is found. Even in classic cryptography, brute force attack is considered time-consuming. These days, this methodology has limited use.

In modern cryptography, the length of a brute force attack depends exponentially on the length of the key. Since modern cryptography uses very long keys, brute force attack is considered inefficient for all practical purposes.

In a Dictionary Attack, the attacker tries a list of known or commonly used passwords, whereas in Brute Force Attack, the attacker does not use a list of passwords; instead, aims at trying all possible combinations in the password space.

Rainbow Table attack

A rainbow table attack is a hacking method that involves the use of a rainbow hash table. Cybercriminals generally favour rainbow table attacks over other types such as dictionary and brute-force attacks because the former allow them to crack passwords faster.

Word List attack

In a dictionary attack, the attacker utilizes a wordlist in the hopes that the user's password is a commonly used word (or a password seen in previous sites). Wordlists aren't restricted to English words; they often also include common passwords (e.g. 'password,' 'letmein,' or 'iloveyou,' or '123456'). List of most common and available wordlists are available freely. One can develop a comprehensive wordlist as per his/her language, purpose and utility.

Chosen plaintext attack

The attacker, in this case, inputs a plaintext and observes the output ciphertext obtained. By examining the plaintext – ciphertext pair, he can easily guess the encryption key. The differential analysis done on RSA algorithm is an example of such attack.

Man in the middle attack

A man in the middle (MITM) attack is a general term for when a perpetrator positions himself in a conversation between a user and an application—either to eavesdrop or to impersonate one of the parties, making it appear as if a normal exchange of information is underway.

Web-based cryptanalysis tools

CrypTool

CrypTool was first launched in 1998. It is an e-learning tool explaining cryptanalysis and cryptography. CrypTool aims at making people understand network security threats and working of cryptology. It includes asymmetric ciphers like RSA, elliptic curve cryptography. CrypTool1 (CT1) experiments with different algorithms and runs on Windows. It was developed in C++ language.

CT2, which was launched in 2014, also runs on Windows. It has an improved GUI and more than hundred cryptological functions. It is developed in .NET &C#. JCrypTool (JCT) which followed CT2 is platform independent.

JCT works on Linux, MacOS, and Windows. JCT is both a function – centric as well as a document – centric tool. In 2009, CrypTool – online (CTO) was launched. CTOconsists of a huge number of encryption methods and analysis tools. It is a web browser based tool and also targeted at smartphones.

EverCrack

An open source GPL software, EverCrack deals chiefly with mono – alphabetic substitution and transposition ciphers. It is a cryptanalysis engine with a multi – language support for English, German, French, Spanish, Italian, Swedish, Dutch and Portuguese. It was initially developed in C language. It is currently concentrating on online web – based applications. Now, the programming is kernel based i.e. deciphering complex ciphers for the kernel.

The overall design goal is to break down complex ciphers systematically into their simplex components for cryptanalysis (by the kernel). The kernel consists of an algebraic design (comparison and reduction) for breaking unilateral, mono – alphabetic ciphers instantaneously. The computational speed is found to be proportional to O (log n).

Cryptol

A software development firm named Galois Inc. developed Cryptol. It is a learning tool as well as a way to analyze algorithms and implementations. Originally designed for NSA, this tool is now used by private firms. The programming language is used for all aspects of developing and using cryptography, such as the design and implementation of new ciphers and the verification of existing cryptographic algorithms.

Cryptol is designed to allow the cryptographer to watch how stream processing functions in the program manipulate the ciphers or encryption algorithms. This aspect of Cryptol has been of particular interest to computer programmers who write new programming languages and to the field of artificial intelligence.

Cryptol deals with cryptographic routines rather than entire cryptographic suites. It was designed for efficiently implementing cryptographic algorithms in hardware circuits. Despite its flaws, the tool can help improve the trustworthiness of many cryptographic algorithms.

AlphaPeeler

AlphaPeeler is a freeware / non-commercial software product for educational and personal use.Its development started in 1997, and AlphaPeeler 1.0 was deployed in June 1998. It includes MD5, SHA – 1, RSA key generation, RIPEMD – 16, etc. Classic ciphers like Playfair are studied here.

AlphaPeeler Professional 1.0 beta was released on 4th July 2001 in public domain. AlphaPeeler was founded with a specific goal of providing the most up-to-date research to assist enterprises, vendors, and carriers to secure their business and development environment. AlphaPeeler development group also creates a wide range of software technology solutions listed in services section such as software development, system analysis and design, documentation and graphic designing.

Crypto Bench

Crypto Bench is a software that performs various cryptanalytic functions. It can generate 14 cryptographic hashes and two checksums. It can encrypt with 29 different secret key or symmetric schemes. It can Encrypt, Decrypt, Sign, and Verify with six different public key or asymmetric schemes.

Ganzúa

Ganzúa (the Spanish word for lockpick) is a cryptanalysis tool for monoalphabetic and polyalphabetic ciphers that can work with almost any set of characters. It is a Java application; it may be executed on Mac OS X, Linux or Windows.

Ganzúa is provided with features to cryptanalysemonoalphabetic and polyalphabetic ciphers. It is Java based, and version 1.01 is available in English and Spanish. In monoalphabetic ciphers, we have alphabet wide substitution tools for Caesar shift cipher. Also, relative frequencies of characters, bigrams and trigrams can be obtained and displayed.

Similarly, for polyalphabetic ciphers, alphabet-wide substitution tools for the Vigenère or Alberti ciphers are available. Relative frequencies for each alphabet is calculated and displayed here as well. Kasiski test is performed on cryptograms.

For both kinds of ciphers, the alphabet used is arbitrary for both plaintext and ciphertext. Indexes of coincidence of cryptograms and languages are calculated. Based on the index of coincidence of the ciphertext and language, the number of alphabets needed to generate a cryptogram is found out. Enforced injective character substitution is carried out. Save and load features are available for ongoing projects.

Elcomsoft Distributed Password Recovery

Elcomsoft Distributed Password Recovery (EPDR) installs "agents" on as many computers as possible. These agents use brute force attack to recover the lost password. EPDR is useful for recovering Office passwords (Office 97/2000/2003/XP) for Word and Excel documents.

Advanced Archive Password Recovery

Advanced Archive Password Recovery supports the dictionary based attacks, plaintext attacks and the brute – force attacks. It has a multilingual interface and strong AES encryption support. Passwords for .zip, .arj , .rar& .ace extensions can be cracked.

Kismet

Kismet is an 802.11b network sniffer and network dissector. It is capable of sniffing using most wireless cards, automatic network IP block detection via UDP, ARP, and DHCP packets, Cisco equipment lists via Cisco Discovery Protocol, weak cryptographic packet logging, and Ethereal and TCP dump compatible packet dump files. It also includes the ability to plot detected networks and estimated network ranges on downloaded maps or user supplied image files.

Lepton's Crack

Lepton's Crack is a generic password cracker. It is easily customizable with a simple plugin system and allows system administrators to review the quality of the passwords being used on their systems. It can perform a dictionary-based (wordlist) attack as well as a brute force (incremental) password scan. It supports standard MD4 hash, standard MD5 hash, NT MD4/Unicode, and Lotus Domino HTTP password (R4) formats.

Crypto Bench

Crypto Bench is a software that performs various cryptanalytic functions. It can generate 14 cryptographic hashes and two checksums. It can encrypt with 29 different secret key or symmetric schemes. It can encrypt, decrypt, sign and verify with six different public key or asymmetric schemes.

17. Porting Details of Mobiles

The porting details of mobile will remain an important ingredient in any investigation by either police or the private investigator. There are many tools offering the services of mobile locations, but most of them provide the details of the SIM issuing location which is based on the first five digits of the 10 digit SIM number. To get the updated porting details of the mobile numbers, one can use the following tools:

The JAS Toolkit.The Toolkit is essential tool for Law Enforcement Officer. This will help with important information immediately on the spot. It is considered a very handy and updated tool.

Features: Offline Cell Id Address Search with display on Google Map. Searching Subscriber Codes. Telephone Code Search like STD | ISD | LRN | VLR | ROAMING CODES | SMS SENDER ID CODES. Cell-Track for monitoring 2G/3G/4G Tower Cell Id for Tower Analysis.

Tower Cell id Info & Tracking is a free software application from the System Maintenance subcategory, part of the System Utilities category. The app is currently available in English and it was last updated on 2020-04-01. The program can be installed on Android. Tower Cell id Info & Tracking (version 3f) has a file size of 6.08 MB and is available for download from their website.

18. Search, Seizure and Cyber Forensics

The search, seizure and cyber forensics of devices are undertaken with regards to legal consequences. The procedure is outlined for preparations and methodology for undertaking the search and seizure for forensics. The investigators if not trained will know the preparations only whereas the investigators who have forensics knowhow/knowledge can undertake the assignment as and when requested by the police in the form of cyber expert. This is included in the book to give an insight to the readers about the processes for search and seizures.

Key points to be kept in mind before undertaking Search and Seizure are explained briefly below:

Preparation: The team ensures readiness of the following-

a) Written directive to undertake search and seizure

b) List of hardware and software to be carried during the search and seizure

c) Seized items/devices chain of custody

d) Prepare a list of questionnaire to be sought from the subject which could be in a statement form.

Operation: Points whilst Search and Seizure is undertaken are as under-

a) Do not forget to search the subject in person for any likely storage drives or memory cards.

b) Raise chain of custody for each device with specifications, serial nos, colour, etc, to be seized

c) Know the limitations of the case. Pen it down to include it in your report.

d) Do not switch off the PC System if it is on and just power down by removing the power supply from the source, if not connected to any external source like UPS or battery. If it is connected to the battery or UPS, just shut down the UPS and battery or pull the cord from the battery terminal. If the system is a laptop, just long press the power on button till the laptop is switched off. In case the private investigator has our snap forensics tool, it can be connected with the system and in couple of minutes removed after extracting the details. Such details should be then hash proved either with available tools and resources or as facilitated by the author of this book.

19. Clone Drives, Compromising Mobiles and PC

Cloning is a process in which bit by bit copy of the content including space is undertaken. Some of the tools are described below:-

a) Acronis It replicates a computer's operating system, software, patches, and drives. It allows you to duplicate the configurations of multiple PC so that each system is identically set up.

Features: It provides a complete image of your PC at a single point in time. This software defines when, what, and where to backup your important data. Acronis secures your important using the stringent security. It offers the easiest way to backup your data and clone disk.

Download link:https://www.acronis.com/en-us/

b) Paragon Drive Copy. It is a professional tool which allows one to migrate disk to a larger drive. It also allows you to manage hard disk partitions effectively.

Features:Users can keep your disk properly organized. This tool enables users to clone their OS to a USB flash drive and use it. Copy or restore files to a hard disk with various sector sizes. It allows the user to perform partitioning operations to keep disks properly organized. This tool has a built-in wizard that restores various types of images.

Download link:https://www.paragon-software.com/

c) O&O. The Disk Image allows you to restore the system and to duplicate or clone hard drive or PC. It supports Windows 10, Windows 8.1, and Windows.

Features: It is easy to restore files, folders, drives, and disk. This software allows you to boost the system with driver integration. It has enhanced functions to control via Command Lines. You can directly create virtual hard disks. This tool provides monitoring and warning of security risks. You can adjust the selected DPI setting of a connected monitor.

Download link: https://www.oo-software.com/en/diskimage-backup-your-data

d) EaseUSTodo Backup. The software product allows you to clone a smaller hard disk drive to a larger hard disk drive. It also allows you to clone HDD to SSD for increasing performance.

Features: It allows you to clone MBR (Master Boot Record) disk to GPT (GUID Partition Table) disk or GPT disk to MBR disk from your small size disk to large size disk. Clone one partition or multiple partitions instead of the whole disk to avoid the loss of your data. This software product helps you to recover deleted data or backup your system. You can restore files, system, partition, or disk.

Download link:https://www.easeus.com/

e) AOMEI Backupper. This app enables you to transfer your operating system to another drive without installing it again. This software helps you to upgrade your hard disk from old disk to a new one.

Features: You can clone one disk to another without a disturbing operating system. Clone data sector by sector. It supports GPT (GUID Partition Table) and MBR (Master Boot Record) partition styles. Clone HDD (Hard Disk Drive) to HDD, HDD to SSD (Solid-State Drive), or SSD to SSD for disk upgrades and data migration. Services are available for Windows 10, Windows 8, Windows, etc.It allows you to access your important files on your tablet, mobile phone, or laptop with your cloud network account.

Download link: https://www.ubackup.com/

f) **Stellar Drive Clone.** It is a tool that enables you to create a replica of your Mac partition and hard drive. It supports FAT-to-FAT, HFS-to-HFS, and NTFS-to-EXFAT cloning. This program can create and store disk images of the hard drive.

Features: You can restore volumes from a disk image file or folder. It enables you to take a backup of important folders and files. The tool is capable to perform cloning of encrypted volumes and hard drive. You can clone hard drive to SSD.

Download link:

https://www.stellarinfo.com/mac-software/clone-mac/clone-mac-drive.php?cjevent=e98e473a7a9411eb814401930a180514

g) Active@ Disk Image. Active@ Disk Image is a handy hard disk image software that helps you to t creates a similar copy of, SSD, USB, HDD, Blu-ray, etc. and stores it into a folder. It is one of the best disk cloning software for Windows 10 that can be used for PC upgrades, clone HDD to SSD, disk duplication or backups, purposes.

Features: This hard drive cloning software supports Windows XP, 7, 8, 10 Vista, Server 2003, and 2012.You can clone disk and mount any image as a virtual drive. This tool provides image compression. A copy of disk partition or hard drives contains only occupied sectors. It offers to image and restore fixed hard disks, and solid-state drives, and removable disks. You can verify the image after creating it.

Download link:https://www.disk-image.com

h) Macrium Reflect 7. Macrium Reflect 7 provides a backup, disk imaging and cloning solution for commercial as well as personal use. This free disk cloning software offers direct disk cloning and a secure way to store your commercial and personal data. You can backup data to local, USB, and networked drives.

Features: It increases the disk space of your computer by rapid delta cloning. Create images of a live/running Windows OS. You can boost your backup in Microsoft Hyper-V virtual machines. This disk imaging software encrypts your backups. Schedule your backup with flexible templates. This HDD to SSD cloning software provides rapid data cloning and restores for fast DR.

Download link: https://www.macrium.com/reflectfree

i) Clonezilla. Clonezilla is a disk imaging or cloning program. It is one of the best disk cloning software which helps you to clone GNU/Linux, Intel-based Mac OS, MS windows, and FreeBSD.

Features: You can clone hard disk and restore one image to multiple local devices. This free hard drive cloning software allows you to restore multiple local devices. This tool supports multicasting. It provides AES-256 encryption to safeguard data access, storage, and transfer.This disk imaging software offers BMR and GPT partition formats of a hard disk.You can clone disk and customize your imaging and cloning.

Download link: https://clonezilla.org/

j) R-Drive Image. R-Drive is a software which provides disk image files creation for duplication and backup process. It contains the exact copy of a hard drive, logical disk, and partition.

Features: You can clone hard disk and store drive image files in removable media such as Iomega Zip, Jazz disks, CD-R(W)/DVD, etc. It creates images without restarting your windows system. The tool can restore images onto their new disks, original disks, hard drive's free space, or partitions. Clone disk by copying data from source disk to the target one. It can connect its image files as read-only virtual drives. This HDD to SSD cloning software has a multi-language user interface.

Download link: https://www.drive-image.com/

k) Driveimage XML. Driveimage XML is another effective software for imaging and backing up the partition and logical drives. It enables you to store images in XML files and process them with 3rd party software.

Features: You can copy directly from one hard disk to another one. This tool lets you clone hard drive, browse images, view, and extract files. You can run DriveImage from runtime WinPE boot CD-ROM or live CD. This disk imaging software provides scheduling automatic backups. It helps you to restore images to the same or a different drive.

Download link: https://www.runtime.org/driveimage-xml.htm

20) Compromising Mobiles

The mobile devices can be compromised by following methodologies:-

a) Installation of applications to access the data on their mobile or on a web portal.

b) By installing applications for viewing the screen of the mobiles.

c) By diverting calls of the mobiles and taking away the OTP for installation of the account held on the victim's mobile in another mobile.

d) By sending phishing links to the victims to take away their account credentials.

e) By compromising the email connected to the google play store or the apple play store.

f) By compromising the Mi account for Mi mobiles.

21) The last four methods involve viewing, extracting or taking away the credentials. The first two methods involve the following steps for android devices:

a) Enabling the developer's option

b) Enabling the third party application installation option

c) Enabling the USB debugger for installation/forensics by USB connections.

22) Applications to compromise mobiles

Some of the mobile applications used to compromise the mobiles are as under:

a) MSpy (https://my.mspyonline.com/)

b) Flexispy (https://www.flexispy.com/)

c)Mobistealth(https://www.mobistealth.com)

d)Highstermobile (https://highstermobile.com)

23) Smartphone Hacking Methodology

The methodologies of hacking smart phones are described briefly as under:-

a) **Compromising a Smartphone** - Advanced security features like disabling the developers option, installing unknown apps by default, protect smartphone models. Apart from these default settings, features like passwords, PIN numbers, finger lock or other biometric features make it all the more difficult for the hacker to install any spyware on the mobile to quite an extent.

b) **Hacking the Camera of a Cell** Phone –There are utilities on github which can be git cloned to use kali linux for creating the links and then sending to the victims to view their camera or audio. The hackers otherwise can access to phone camera and view the pictures stored on the device by compromising the victim's email id. Some phone spy apps software such as Flexispy, mobistealth, highster mobile or mSpy are much easier to use and allow monitoring of multimedia file sharing to recipients on social media platforms. These applications work for targeting either iOS or Android, however, the applications will need to be installed on the victim's mobile.

c) **Hacking an iOS Phone Camera**- The victims with iPhones require the hacker to: Enter iCloud credentials for the device, and complete verifications with the onetime password (OTP). One can then enable the optional back-up feature, to sync the targeted data to the hacker's or laptop. The hacker can then login to the online dashboard and view contents of the phone camera's as stored in the storage. Some dashboards also provide access commands to spy on sharing of social media photos to Twitter, Facebook, and other platforms.

d) **Hacking an Android Phone Camera** –Hackers can access an Android camera by downloading the phone hacking software and installation onto the target device. When notified, the hacker permits all necessary permissions, to enable hacking into an Android OS. In this case too, one can send the link created on Kali Linux with github source code and view the victim without their knowledge.

e) **Hacking a Phone Using the Number**–There are couple of ways by which the hacker can hack a phone. A hacker first obtains the credentials of the victim by means of phishing. He then visits the mobile vendor's official website. After that, he opts for the preferred subscription package for the hacker's requirement. He fills in information about the targeted phone (model number and other details). For iPhone, only the iCloud credentials are required and then verified on the app provider's platform. Once it is done, then clicking the data tab to start the process. He then logs in on the dashboard at app's website, and begin viewing the information of the target phone. This process leads to information of the target phone. The second method is to dial a mobile code on the mobile handset of the victim in which the calls get diverted to another number without the knowledge of the victim. This helps in snatching away the whatsApp kind of apps which has a feature to authenticate the One Time Password over voice calls.

f) **Establishing whether phone is Hacked**–This topic is dealt with different methodologies to establish whether the phone is hacked or not. Following are the indications which may indicate likely a compromise:

i) Go to Settings, check whether the developer's option is enabled or not. In normal android phones, the developer's option is disabled and one will need to click several times to enable it.

ii) One also need to check if the 'install third party applications' are enabled or not.

iii) We also need to see the system aps and other installed apps. Should we find any suspicious app, the same can be checked on the mobile vendor's site for default app confirmation. List of suspicious apps can be easily found for both IOS and android phone. Any app with icon of android will need to be ascertained if it is genuine vendor's app or not.

iv Even with limited phone usage, the battery gets drained faster.

v) The network signal vanishes for longer time indicates SIM swapping.

vi)The location and mobile data may get enabled without any user intervention.

g) **Solution for Hacked Phone**- In case of any suspicion, the credentials of the IOS or Mi account for Mi mobiles should be changed. Similarly many handset brands are now having their own cloud storage. Hackers try to get the credentials and view the usage of the phones. By resorting to factory setting, the hacked mobiles cannot be safe. The procedure to make it safe is also explained as under:-

i) Make an email id preferably without any mobile SIM (as of now it is possible for gmail).

ii) Open your old (presumably hacked email) and go to settings and forward email option.

iii) Add the new email id which was created in step (i). Authenticate it.

iv) Login to your new email id and go to the settings and then to general tab and add the old email id in the 'send mail as'.

v) Format the handset after saving important documents and add the new email id only.

vi) Now one can see the mail of the old email id forwarded in the new email id. One can also respond to the old email id without login, by the new email is in send mail option which will start showing the old email id as well. Select the old email id and one can send the email from there.

24. Social Engineering & Art of Information Gathering

It's a saying "Information is wealth!". The very first stage in Ethical Hacking and cyber security is Information gathering. Information gathering is a phase in which maximum amount of information is collected of the particular target. This information helps the attacker to analyze and understand the target much better. When it comes to personal information, it may include name, birthday, mobile number, vehicle number, job location, residential address etc. When it comes to corporate information it may include website, email address, sub domains, way back machine records etc.

Information gathering not only helps to understand the target better but also helps to find weakness and vulnerable points in accordance with the target. It makes the process of attack much simple to execute.

In order to facilitate the process of recon and information gathering, a common but most powerful tactic is used. It is Social Engineering. Social engineering involves manipulating and fooling the human mind with an intention to obtain informational or sensitive information.

Social engineering is the most powerful tactic followed in today's times and can reveal a lot of information and sensitive details about a particular target. There are various methodologies under social engineering such as:

Quid Pro Quo – when an attacker pretends to help the target in the name of technical or tech support and eventually gains access over the target's system is called as Quid Pro Quo.

Tailgating – when an attacker uses other's property or identity to obtain unauthorized information or to gain restricted access is Tailgating. Common example is when an attacker uses RFID card of other person to enter unauthorized area.

Pretexting – it involves adapting a completely new digital identity. It means when someone uses non-real identity in the digital world in order to betray trust and lure the audience.

Impersonation- when someone performs identity theft by using other person's name and position to attack and access the sensitive information. Social engineering is not only involved in the digital world but is a part of everyday life cycle. When a person even tries to peep into the password it's called as shoulder surfing. Advance social engineering attacks includes phishing, vishing, smishiing and whaling.

It is very important to understand the human psychology. By information gathering we can easily identity the likes, dislikes, personality, engagements and activeness of a person and thus this information can help us to play with cyber psychology of the person and lure to fall in the attacker's trap.

Social media impersonation, cyber bullying, free gifts and offers, fake bank calls, spam job alerts, email containing luring attachments are best real time examples of social engineering attacks.

25. Data Recovery

According to the technical definition in computing, data recovery is a process of salvaging inaccessible, lost, corrupted, damaged or formatted data from secondary storage, removable media or files, when the data stored in them cannot be accessed in a usual way. Whenever a file is deleted from a computer, it actually doesn't really get deleted in that sense. There is a file allocation index table created by the hard disk. Whenever a file is deleted, the index linking to that file via the hard disk is erased and the space becomes unallocated. However, the RAW file of the original file still remains unless and until a new few file is over written in that same location of the deleted file. Data recovery in simple terms is the process of recovering the original files via the RAW file of the deleted one.

RAW file is the original file itself. However, the percentage of recovery actually depends on the amount of data overwritten at those locations of the deleted files.

Lesser the data is overwritten; more is the possibility of data recovery. There are various data recovery tools which recovers the data but most of them are paid such as Tenor Data Recovery and Stellar Data Recovery Suite. Among all these, Recuva is a completely free software through which data recovery can be done. It's a small and simple application but is highly preferred and effective in terms of recovering the data. It has quick scan as well as deep scan to actually dig deep for the RAW files and analyze the deleted data.

https://www.ccleaner.com/recuva

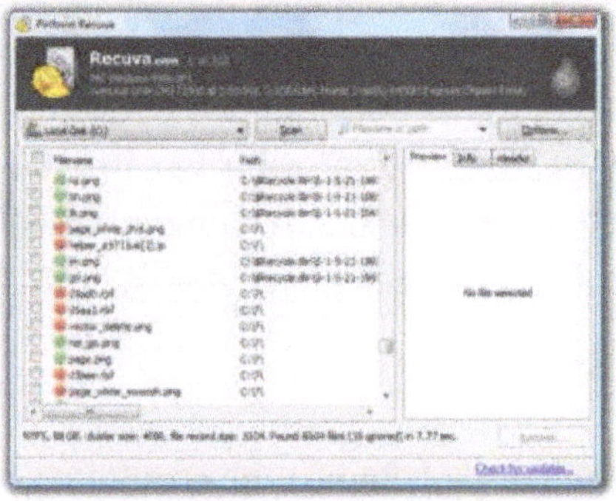

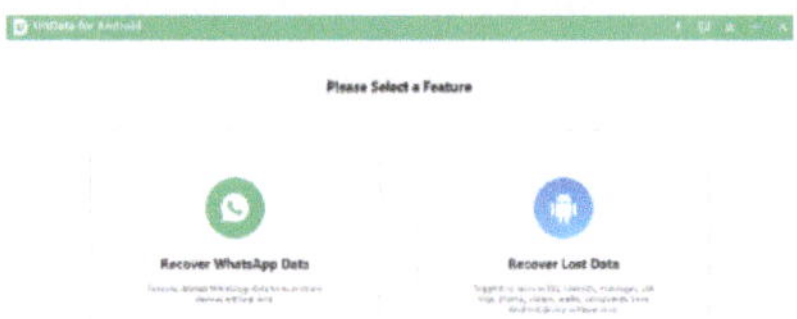

There is also a paid version for this software but the freeware version also does equally good job with high accuracy but one is limited to extract the deleted data in the free version.

Apart from windows data recovery, android data recovery also is possible. Android data recovery is bit more sophisticated and difficult as newer smartphones have strict security settings in their operating systems. Administrative level changes are only possible when the device is actually rooted or jail broken. However, there are a variety of tools available for Android Data Recovery. One of them is ULT Data android recovery which not only helps to recover deleted data from android but also has a feature to recover deleted Whatsapp messages.

Other Data Recovery Software as per Wikipedia

Four phases of data recovery

Usually, there are four phases when it comes to successful data recovery, though that can vary depending on the type of data corruption and recovery required.

Phase 1 Repair the hard disk drive. The hard drive is repaired in order to get it running in some form, or at least in a state suitable for reading the data from it. For example, if heads are bad they need to be changed; if the PCB is faulty then it needs to be fixed or replaced; if the spindle motor is bad the platters and heads should be moved to a new drive.

Phase 2 Image the drive to a new drive or a disk image file. When a hard disk drive fails, the importance of getting the data off the drive is the top priority. The longer a faulty drive is used, the more likely further data loss is to occur. Creating an image of the drive will ensure that there is a secondary copy of the data on another device, on which it is safe to perform testing and recovery procedures without harming the source.

Phase 3 Logical recovery of files, partition, MBR and filesystem structures. After the drive has been cloned to a new drive, it is suitable to attempt the retrieval of lost data. If the drive has failed logically, there are a number of reasons for that. Using the clone it may be possible to repair the partition table or master boot record (MBR) in order to read the file system's data structure and retrieve stored data.

Phase 4 Repair damaged files that were retrieved. Data damage can be caused when, for example, a file is written to a sector on the drive that has been damaged. This is the most common cause in a failing drive, meaning that data needs to be reconstructed to become readable. Corrupted documents can be recovered by several software methods or by manually reconstructing the document using a hex editor.

Data recovery cannot always be done on a running system. In such a case, a boot disk, live CD, live USB, or any other type of live distrowhich contains a minimal operating system would suffice.

- BartPE: a lightweight variant of Microsoft Windows XP or Windows Server 2003 32-bit operating systems, similar to a Windows Preinstallation Environment, which can be run from a live CD or live USB drive. Discontinued.
- Finnix: a Debian-based Live CD with a focus on being small and fast, useful for computer and data rescue
- Disk Drill Basic: capable of creating bootable Mac OS X USB drives for data recovery
- Knoppix: contains utilities for data recovery under Linux
- SpinRite: a FreeDOS-based data recovery tool for hard disks and magnetic storage devices
- SystemRescueCD: an Arch Linux based live CD, useful for repairing unbootable computer systems and retrieving data after a system crash
- Windows Pre-installation Environment (WinPE): A customizable Windows Boot DVD (made by Microsoft and distributed for free). Can be modified to boot to any of the programs listed.

Consistency checkers

- CHKDSK: a consistency checker for DOS and Windows systems
- Disk First Aid: a consistency checker for Mac OS 9
- Disk Utility: a consistency checker for Mac OS X
- fsck: a consistency checker for UNIX
- gparted: a GUI for GNU parted, the GNU partition editor, capable of calling fsck

File recovery

- CDRoller: recovers data from optical disc
- Data Recovery Wizard: Windows file recovery utility by EaseUS
- Disk Drill Basic: data recovery application for Mac OS X and Windows
- dvdisaster: generates error-correction data for optical discs
- GetDataBack: a Windows recovery program
- Hetman Partition Recovery: data drive recovery solution
- IsoBuster: recovers data from optical discs, USB sticks, flash drives and hard drives
- Mac Data Recovery Guru: Mac OS X data recovery program which works on USB sticks, optical media, and hard drives
- MiniTool Partition Wizard: for Windows 7 and later; includes data recovery
- Norton Utilities: a suite of utilities that has a file recovery component
- PhotoRec: advanced multi-platform program with text-based user interface used to recover files
- Recover My Files: proprietary software for Windows 2000 and later—FAT, NTFS and HFS
- Recovery Toolbox: freeware and shareware tools plus online services for various Windows 2000 and later programs
- Recuva: proprietary software for Windows 2000 and later—FAT and NTFS
- Stellar Data Recovery for Mac: data recovery utility for Mac OS
- Stellar Data Recovery for Windows: data recovery utility for Windows

- Stellar Photo Recovery: photo recovery utility for Mac OS and Windows
- TestDisk: free, open source, multi-platform. recover files and lost partitions
- TotalRecovery: bootable backup and recovery system for Windows
- TuneUp Utilities: a suite of utilities that has a file recovery component for Windows XP and later
- Windows File Recovery: a command-line utility from Microsoft to recover deleted files for Windows 10 version 2004 and later ()
- Wondershare Recoverit Data Recovery: data recovery utility for Mac OS and Windows (https://recoverit.wondershare.net/)

26) Some other useful data recovery tools are:

- 7 data recovery suite
- Ease US Data Recovery
- Laptop Data Rescue
- Power Data Recovery
- SP Windows data recovery
- Windows password reset and recovery

27) Hashing

Hashing is the transformation of a string of characters into a usually shorter fixed-length value or key that represents the original string. Hashing is done to validate the data integrity of the files and documents. There are many types of hash algorithms as explained below:

- **MD5**. The MD5 algorithm encodes a string of information into a 128-bit fingerprint. It's one of the oldest and most widely-used hashing algorithms in the world, but it is also starting to show its age in the form of a high risk of hash collision.

- **SHA-2.** Developed by the NSA, this cryptographic hash function builds on the older SHA-1 algorithm. Both the current algorithm and its predecessor use six hashing algorithms in 244-, 256-, 384-, or 512-bit configurations.
- **CRC32.** "CRC" stands for "cyclical reduction check." It's a kind of code used to discover errors or changes in a data set. Mostly used in zip files or for file integrity checks, CRC32 produces the same hashed output every time it is run.
- **RipeMD.** Available in multiple bit configurations with 160-bit the most popular, RipeMD is a cryptographic hashing algorithm that is used in the Bitcoin standard. Other cryptocurrencies use it as well.
- **Tiger**. Tiger is a hash function invented to work with 64-bit platforms. Available in 128-bit and 160-bit configurations, Tiger has no distinguishing initializing values. It appends a byte with hexadecimal value 0x01. A variation, Tiger2, appends a byte with hexadecimal value 0x08.
- **xxHash**. xxHash is a non-cryptographic hash function known for its exceptional speed, working at RAM speed limits. The most up-to-date variation, XXH3, performs exceptionally well with small data.
- **BCrypt.** This hash function is designed to be slow, with the intention of making password cracking more time consuming and discouraging cybercriminals attempting to execute quick attacks.
- **Argon2**. Argon2 uses an "adaptive" hashing algorithm that can be calibrated with a "work factor," making the hash more or less complicated.

The most common hash values for data integrity are as under:

Hash Value	Length	Character
MD5	16	32
SHA1	20	40
SHA256	32	64
SHA384	48	96
SHA512	64	126

Hashing Tools/Links(https://www.binaryfortress.com/HashTools)

Hashing is a process to establish file integrity for legal and forensics purposes. A portable free version of Hash Tool for Windows is from Binary Fortress Software.

For text hash generator:

https://www.browserling.com/tools/all-hashes

For online file hash generator:

https://www.pelock.com/products/hash-calculator

28) Document Meta Data

The exif details or the meta data establishes the creation date of the document besides the ownership of the document.

"EXIF Data" can be an important source to find out the GPS location, camera type, model no. of phone, date &time , size of photo, longitude, latitude information etc.

Some tools from which we can get Exif data of any image:

Philharvy :https://exiftool.org/
JPEG Snoop :https://jpegsnoop.en.softonic.com/

www.metapicz.com
www.veraxif.com/en/

29) CDR Analysis

The short form CDR is often used and is the abbreviation for Call Data Records. It contains vital information of the caller and receiver including the IP address.

The nomenclature of the mobile related identification features are as under:

IMSI = **International Mobile Subscriber Identity**. This is a unique identifier that defines a subscriber in the wireless world, including the country and mobile network to which the subscriber belongs. It has the format MCC-MNC-MSIN. MCC = Mobile Country Code (e.g. 310 for USA); MNC = Mobile Network Code (e.g. 410 for AT&T), MSIN = sequential serial number. All signalling and messaging in GSM and UMTS networks uses the IMSI as the primary identifier of a subscriber. The IMSI is one of the pieces of information stored on a SIM card.

ICCID = **Integrated Circuit Card ID**. This is the identifier of the actual SIM card itself - i.e. an identifier for the SIM chip. It is possible to change the information contained on a SIM (including the IMSI), but the identify of the SIM itself remains the same.

IMEI is short

for **International Mobile Equipment Identity** and is a unique number given to every single mobile phone, typically found behind the battery. IMEI numbers of cellular

phones connected to a GSM network are stored in a database (EIR - Equipment Identity Register) containing all valid mobile phone equipment. When a phone is reported stolen or is not type approved, the number is marked invalid.

MSISDN = **Mobile Station ISDN number**. This is the full phone number of a subscriber, including the national country code (e.g. 1 for US, 44 for UK, etc.). The purpose of the MSISDN is simply to allow a device to be called. A subscriber can have multiple MSISDNs (e.g. one phone number for business, one for personal calls, one for fax, etc.), but generally only one IMSI. The MSISDN does not need to be stored on the SIM card. In cases where it is stored on the SIM, the main reason is so that the user can use check to see what their own MSISDN is (in case they forget). The MSISDN is never signalled to or from the device.

IMSI has 15 digits

ICCID has between 19 and 20 digits

IMEI has a "unique" 15 digit number

ICCID identified the unique physical SIM chip. IMSI indentified the SIM as unique in International Network. The SIM card may change the information including IMSI stored in it but ICCID cannot be changed.

The **ICCID (Integrated Circuit Card ID)** is an 18- or 19-digit identification number used to identify the SIM itself. The IMSI (International Mobile Subscriber Identity) is a code used by the phone company to identify the SIM on the mobile network. The IMEI (International Mobile Station Equipment Identity) is an international "Serial number" for your phone (device itself) to properly identify it on the carriers network.

ICCID (Integrated Circuit Card Identifier) identifies each SIM internationally.

IMSI-International mobile Subscriber Identity is used to identify the user of a cellular network and is a unique identification associated with all cellular networks. It is stored as a 64 bit field and is sent by the phone to the network. It is also used for acquiring other details of the mobile in the HLR or as locally copied in the Visitor Location Register.

IMEI - International Mobile Station Equipment Identity is a unique number, used to identify mobile phones, as well as some satellite phones. It is usually found printed inside the battery compartment of the phone, but can also be displayed on-screen on most phones by entering *#06# on the dialpad, or alongside other system information in the settings menu on smart phones operating systems.

The format of the ICCID is: MMCC IINN NNNN NNNN NN C x

MM = Constant (ISO 7812 Major Industry Identifier)

CC = Country Code

II= Issuer Identifier

N{12} = Account ID ("SIM number")

C = Checksum calculated from the other 19 digits using the Luhn algorithm.

x= An extra 20th digit is returned by the 'AT!ICCID?' command, but it is not officially part of the ICCID.

If you need to check your Country and International Phone code with the ICCID number you can use our ICCID CHECKER

Other abbreviations:

MOC = Mobile Originating Call, MTC = Mobile Terminating Call, PRO = PRI Outgoing, PRT = PRI Incoming, SMO = SMS Originating, SMT=SMS Terminating, CFW = Call Forwarding, PP = Prepaid, PO = Postpaid, N/A=Not Available in CDR, 2G:- 2G-Voice Call/2G-SMS, 3G:- 3G-Voice Call/3G-SMS, 3GV:- 3G-Video Call, 4G:- 4G-Voice Call/4G-SMS, TOTAL VOLUME = Download Volume + Upload Volume, GPD = General Packet Data, AOCHATM = App Originating Chat Message, ATCHATM= App Terminating Chat Message, AOCONM = App Originating Contact Message, ATCONM = App Terminating Contact Message,

AOFILEM = App Originating File Message, ATFILEM = App Terminating File Message, AOINVITEREG = App Originating Invite Message, ATINVITEREG = App Terminating Invite Message" AOIVRREG = App Originating OTP Via IVR, ATIVRREG = App Terminating OTP Via IVR, AOLOCM=App Originating Location Message, ATLOCM = App Terminating Location Message, AOPICM = App Originating Picture Message, ATPICM = App Terminating Picture Message, ATPSTN = App Incoming PSTN, AOPSTN = App Outgoing PSTN, ATSMS = App Incoming SMS, AOSMS = App Outgoing SMS, AOSMSREG = App Originating OTP Via SMS, ATSMSREG = App Terminating OTP Via SMS, AOVIDEO = App Originating Video Call, ATVIDEO = App Terminating Video Call, AOVIDM = App Originating Video Message, ATVIDM = App Terminating Video Message, AOVOICE = App Originating Voice Call, ATVOICE = App Terminating Voice Call, AOVOICEM = App Originating Audio Message, ATVOICEM = App Terminating Audio Message

Mobile SIMs have 10 digit numbers like 7769823817. The first part consisting 5 digits are called 'Mobile Switching Centre Code' and the last part consisting 5 digits are called 'Subscriber Number'.

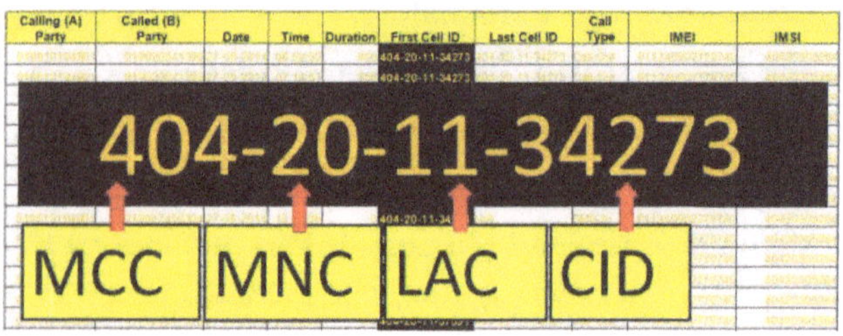

A GSM Cell ID (CID) is a generally unique number used to identify each Base transceiver station (BTS) or sector of a BTS within a Location area code (LAC) if not within a GSM network. The last digit of CID represents cells' Sector ID

Value 0 is used for omni-directional antenna.

Value 1, 2, 3 are used to identify sectors of tri-sector or bisector antennas.

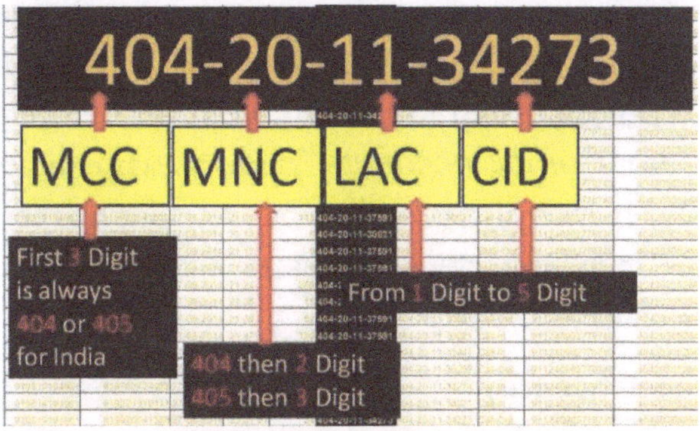

Cell Global Identity / Identifier

MCC + MNC + LAC + CID = CGI

If the duration is 0 or 1, it pertains to SMS. There are no missed call indications.

Different First Cell ID and Last Cell ID indicates the subject was moving while the call was made.

30) Email Security

Email security is a term for any procedure that protects email content and accounts against unauthorized access. Email service providers have email security measures in place to secure client accounts and information from hackers. It's used in doing cyber investigations as it's a part of it.

Email Security requirement

Email protection is important because of cyber threats like social attacks that target organizations via email (and other communication channels). For example, phishing emails might trick users into giving up sensitive information, approving fake invoices, or downloading malware that can go on to infect your network. To understand what is email security properly, why and when one needs it. An email is a window that hackers use to penetrate your computer systems. Just as you have insect screens on windows to prevent pests from entering your home, *you can install software to secure the access and content of your email accounts.* Such collective measures define email security. Individuals, as well as business organizations, can use these services to protect overall access to either one or their entire enterprise accounts.

Types of Email Security

Email Security Features are -

a) Spam Filters. A significant proportion of emails that you receive daily are marketing emails.

b) Anti-virus Protection. Spam filters play the role of separating the spam emails from the regular ones.

c) Image & Content Control. Hackers use emails for phishing purposes.

d) Data Encryption.

Securing Emails

The following are the methods to secure emails.

Login to email>>Click the Settings icon on the right hand side>>Click on all Settings

a) Click on 'Forwarding and POP/IMAP'

i) Check the email forwarding option>>disable it if it is enabled as it is being forwarded to another email (and the email id would be mentioned which will need to be removed after taking the screenshot) and click on save changes.

ii) Check the POP download>>disable it if it is enabled and click on save changes.

iii) Check the IMAP Access>>disable it if it is enabled and click on save changes.

Checking Activity and IP address?

Many of us do not know how to check our own activity and IP address of email. But we can find the following details.

Access Type [?] (Browser, mobile, POP3, etc.)	**Location (IP address)** [?]	**Date/Time** (Displayed in your time zone)

It is very easy to find the details, we just need to click on "Details" which is found on the right hand side at the very bottom of the mail box and the above details can be found. The hacker's address and contact details can be found by this ip which is not recognized.

Compromising Emails

The email can be exploited by hackers very easily even if the access is given for five minutes.

a) Adding unknown or hacker's email ids in the email forwarding option. The hackers can continue to view the emails even if the actual user changes his/her password.

b) The hacker can continue to check on your location through find my device option if he has your email password.

c) The hacker can check all the user's photographs, documents and videos of the android device by checking the Google drive of the connected email id. This aspect is not limited to the user's handset usage, but also the details/data of the previous handset too.

SPF

Sender Policy Framework (SPF) hardens your DNS servers and restricts who can send emails from your domain. SPF can prevent domain spoofing. It enables your mail server to determine when a message came from the domain that it uses. SPF has three major elements: a policy framework as its name implies, an authentication method and specialized headers in the actual email itself that convey this information.

To create the SPF, follow these five simple steps.

Step 1: Gather IP addresses that are used to send email. The first step to implement **SPF** is to identify which mail servers you use to send email from your domain.

Step 2: Make a list of your sending domains.

Step 3: **Create** your **SPF** record.

Step 4: Publish your **SPF** to DNS.

SPF check

SPF helps receiving servers verify that mail sent from your domain is actually from your organization, and is sent by a mail server authorized by you. **SPF** helps deliver messages to recipients' inboxes— **SPF** helps prevent messages from your domain from being delivered to spam.

SPF breaks when a message is forwarded. **SPF does** nothing to protect brands against cybercriminals who spoof the display name or "**header** from" address in their message, which is the more frequently spoofed "from" address since it's the address most visible to the email recipient.

SPF Prevents Spoofing

An **SPF** TXT record is a DNS record that helps **prevent spoofing** and phishing by verifying the domain name from which email messages are sent. **SPF** validates the origin of email messages by verifying the IP address of the sender against the alleged owner of the sending domain.

DKIM

DomainKeys Identified Mail, or DKIM, is a technical standard that helps protect email senders and recipients from spam, spoofing, and phishing. It is a form of email authentication that allows an organization to claim responsibility for a message in a way that can be validated by the recipient.

DKIM (DomainKeys Identified Mail) is an email security standard designed to make sure messages aren't altered in transit between the sending and recipient servers. It uses public-key cryptography to sign email with a private key as it leaves a sending server.

Setting up DKIM

Steps to set up DKIM

a) Generate the domain key for your domain.

b) Add the public key to your domain's DNS records. Email servers can use this key to verify your messages' DKIM signatures.

c) Turn on DKIM signing to start adding a DKIM signature to all outgoing messages.

DKIM verification

Onecancheck/validate your DKIM record by using DKIMrecordChecker.

a) Enter 'Google' as the Selector. As an example, we're using a generated domain key from Google Apps.

b) The DKIM record is correctly configured when the DKIM Checker shows 'This is a valid DKIM key record'. ...

c) If the selector is not valid.

When **DKIM** alignment **fails**—or when the d= value in the Header From does not match the d= value in the **DKIM** signature—it can negatively impact deliverability as mailbox providers may send the message to the spam folder or block it entirely.

DomainKeys Identified Mail, or DKIM, is a technical standard that helps protect email senders and recipients from spam, spoofing, and phishing. It is a form of email authentication that allows an organization to claim responsibility for a message in a way that can be validated by the recipient.

DKIM and Digital Signature

DomainKeys Identified Mail (**DKIM**) allows senders to associate a domain name with an email message, thus vouching for its authenticity. A sender creates the **DKIM** by "**signing**" the email with a digital **signature**. This "**signature**" is located in the message's header.

DKIM keys

When enabling **DKIM**, there is a private key stored on your server and a public key that is stored in the DNS.

DKIM keys do not expire, but you should rotate them periodically (we suggest every 12 months)

DMARC

Domain-based Message Authentication, Reporting and Conformance (DMARC) ties the first two protocols together with a consistent set of policies. It also links the sender's domain name with what is listed in the ***From:*** header and also has some better reporting back from mail recipients.

DMARC Utility

DMARC makes it easier for Internet Service Providers (ISPs) to prevent malicious email practices, such as domain spoofing in order to phish for recipients' personal information. Essentially, it allows email senders to specify how to handle emails that were not authenticated using SPF or DKIM.

What is DMARC and how does it work?

Domain-based Message Authentication, Reporting, and Conformance, or DMARC, is a technical standard that helps protect email senders and recipients from spam, spoofing, and phishing. Specifically, DMARC establishes a method for a domain owner to: Publish its email authentication practices.

DMARC record

DMARC, which stands for Domain-based Message Authentication, Reporting, and Conformance, is a DNS TXT Record that can be published for a domain to control what happens if a message fails authentication (i.e. the recipient server can't verify that the message's sender is who they say they are).

Requirement of DMARC, SPF and DKIM

Phishing and email spam are the biggest opportunities for hackers to enter the network. If a single user clicks on some malicious email attachment, it can compromise an entire enterprisewith ransomware cryptojacking scripts, data leakages or privilege escalation exploits. What isn't as well known is why most enterprises need all three of these protocols to protect their email infrastructures. Like much in the IT world, the multiple solutions don't all necessarily overlap. Actually, they are quite complementary to each other, and chances are good that the average business will need all three of them.

31) Revealing Instagram and FB account

Social media are the best locations to find potential and active information about a particular target or an organization. However, despite of numerous social media platforms, Instagram and Facebook are the two major platforms where there is maximum probability of target account being existed.

Even an inactive and less digital person does have an Instagram or a Facebook account registered. These two sources are main objective of an attacker to find potential information. There are various ways to do such but one of the most common and manual method is to actually enter either the mobile number or email address of the person in the Forgot Password option. Whenever a person forgets the password, Facebook sends an email or SMS notification to the person regarding password reset instructions. It only happens when there is an account created with the given email address or mobile number, if the reset instructions are given, it's simple means that there is a Facebook account present on the given mobile or email. The same method can be applied on Instagram as well as other famous social media platforms.

Once we identity that the person is present on Facebook or Instagram, then we can directly search them using their profile picture or name. At times target also keeps email and mobile number information as open. In the investigator is not able to get the full mobile numbers or email ids, the same can be searched on other social media sites to find the matching mobile ending and email. Email can also be guessed as per the number of characters displayed.

The below methodology shows how by using an email address we can reach to target's Facebook account.

Method 1.

a) Logout from your gmail on your browser

b) Go to forgot password>>put the email ids of the subject>>get the mobile ending number and alternate/original email hints

c) Search as per criminal profiling with the name and businesses associated

d) Get the complete number and alternate emails

e) Search for the person on the facebook forgot email/password page>>one will get the associated facebook profile.

f) Go to google from different browser>>Go to the gmail login page and put the mobile number>>get the type of handset and additional details. Do not forget to take screenshots. Save all details and screenshots in a specifically marked folder for the case.

Method 2.(For FB harassments)

a) Login on the facebook account of the victim on the laptop.

b) In another laptop login on the facebook account of the informer or who has received the message regarding the victim.

c) Now check and note down the names of the person who is common on both the facebook accounts opened on two different laptops in the notification display on known person/s. There could be one or two common profiles of the suspect/s.

d) Then proceed as Method 1 to get the details.

32) Alternate Emails/Contact Details Finding

This aspect is very useful to find details of the missing or absconding persons even if they change their handsets and/or SIM numbers. Police can generally find the details of the new SIMs on the same handset by IMEI numbers. Now the real problem arises when the subject changes the handset. The new SIMs on the changed handset by the same subject can be found partly by CDR (the subject generally checks the call and number correctness on their old SIMs before discarding it. This aspect is recorded in the CDR and can assist one to get some clue). The confirmation of the new SIMs can then be established by going to the recovery mode of the email and social media accounts wherein the investigator can get the new number's ending.

33) Bluetooth or Wi-Fi Pairing

Bluetooth and Wi-Fi pairing information is also very valuable to get the evidential information about the person who was present with his/her device on that particular date and time. The pairing information can be found out either by undertaking a mobile forensics or laptop forensics. The tool exists for getting the information whether the victim/suspect visited certain person. Once this information is available, one can undertake complete forensics of that particular laptop or mobile. The identification of the device paired on a particular data and time will be able to prove whether the person was present at the crime scene on that particular date and time.

34) Compromising What's App and Signal Apps

WhatsApp is used by a large number of users. The data is generally not stored on the server of the whatsApp, however, the data collected from the user could be used for either marketing or OSINT purposes by their partners. An investigator can get any user's data only from either the handset of the user or from their google drive in case of android. Signal messenger application is also similar to WhatsApp however the make and features are a bit different. There are seven methods by which one can get the details/data of any user of such apps. The methodologies as under:

a) QR code: www.webwhatsapp.com (Data can be pulled)

The data of mobiles are on handset and the servers have handshaking features. By going to the website, one will find the QR code which is required to be scanned by the mobile device whose data is to be pulled. One can open the whatsApp on the mobile and go to the three dots to view the whatsApp web. If it shows logged in to a device, it means that some other device can view the whatsApp of the person and if the scanner pops up to scan the QR code, that means the device is not hacked by this methodology.

b) By dialling the mobile code for call diversion.

In this methodology, one can dial the code for diverting all the calls to another specific number. When this is done, the hacker then tries to install the victim's whatsApp on another device and opts for verification by call. This is best achieved when the victim is generally asleep so that if the code comes by the SMS, no action is taken. Once the hacker hears the code by call diversion, he immediately provides it for instant verification and thereafter, the victim is logged out of his/her whatsApp and the hacker can then change the number of the victim which was connected with the whatsApp to his own. This results in permanent loss of the whatsApp account. The victim is left to file a cyber complaint and seek expert advice to find out which number is now connected with his/her whatsApp account. To do this, one can inform the admin of various groups to seek verification of the changed number as indicate and assist the victim with the information. Social engineering tactics can also be explored to get the real identify of the hacker. In this procedure, the hacker cannot pull the old data, but can interact with the victim's associates, more so in whatsApp groups to gather information to achieve his objective. Victim's phone is required for couple of seconds. This method is best done in late nights.

c) OTP installation methods.

In this method, the hacker somehow tries to convince the victim to share his/her OTP for verification. Hacker generally poses as the security department's of the whatsApp to convince the victim to share the code to verify the correct users as he can see two device using the same whatsApp. The victim gets alarmed and easily provides the code thinking that the other unknown user will be logged off. The hacker then installs whatsApp on another device and uses the same code to permanently steal away the victim's whatsApp. In this type of attack, the hacker cannot gain access to the pervious data but only the new or unread conversations can be seen.

d) By installing applications through social engineering

The hacker convinces the victim to install some malicious applications which can compromise the victim's mobile and the hacker can view the messages. The applications could be any screen forwarding applications available on the google play store.

e) By Phishing Links after compromising email password/Gdrive access

The hacker can send phishing links to the victim to compromise his/her email password and gain access to the Gdrive to get the whatsApp backup from the drive.

f) By Cloning the Mobile through enabled NFC

The hacker takes advantage of enabled NFC of the victim's mobile and tries to clone the mobile as is done on data transfer from the old mobile to the new one. In this case, the whatsapp has been found to be running on both the mobile handsets simultaneously, however the messages are received on that handset whose whatsapp application is accessed. The other handset doesn't get messages, but it remains connected to the whatsapp as well.

g) By Spy applications

By installing the spy applications (freely available) on the victim's mobile handset, one can get the whatsapp messages and view it.

35) Evidence Gathering, Preserving and Presenting

Digital evidence is volatile and fragile and the improper handling of this evidence can alter it. Because of its volatility and fragility, protocols need to be followed to ensure that data is not modified during its handling (i.e., during its access, collection, packaging, transfer, and storage). These protocols delineate the steps to be followed when handling digital evidence. There are four phases involved in the initial handling of digital evidence: identification, collection, acquisition, and preservation (ISO/IEC 27037; as amplified in Cybercrime Module 4 on Introduction to Digital Forensics).

There are protocols for the collecting volatile evidence. Volatile evidence should be collected based on the order of volatility; that is, the most volatile evidence should be collected first, and the least volatile should be collected last. In accordance with the ISO/IEC 27037, following are important ingredients to be kept in mind:

- registers, cache
- routing table, ...[address resolution protocol or ARP] cache, process table, kernel statistics, memory
- temporary file systems
- disk
- remote logging and monitoring data that is relevant to the system in question
- physical configuration, network topology
- archival media

In the identification phase, preliminary information is obtained about the cybercrime case prior to collecting digital evidence. This preliminary information is similar to that which is sought during a traditional criminal investigation. The investigator seeks to answer the following questions:

- Who was involved?
- What happened?
- When did the cybercrime occur?
- Where did the cybercrime occur?
- How did the cybercrime occur?

The answers to these questions will provide investigators with guidance on how to proceed with the case.

Evidence preservation is the process of seizing suspect property without altering or changing the contents of data that resides on devices and removable media. It is the first step in digital evidence recovery. A chain of custody of the evidence is a mandatory requirement.

The actual collection of the evidence involves the preservation of volatile evidence and the powering down of digital devices. The state of operation of the digital devices encountered will dictate the collection procedures. For instance, if a computer is encountered, if the device is on, volatile evidence (e.g., temporary files, register, cache, and network status and connections, to name a few) is preserved before powering down the device and collecting it. There are circumstances where digital devices will not and cannot be collected (e.g., due to size and/or complexity of the systems and/or their hardware and software configurations, because these systems provide critical services)

In these situations, volatile and non-volatile data are collected through special procedures that require live acquisition.

As far as acquisition is concerned, different approaches to performing acquisition exist. The approach taken depends on the type of digital device. For example, the procedure for acquiring evidence from a computer hard drive is different from the procedure required to obtain digital evidence from mobile devices, such as smartphones.

Unless live acquisition is performed, evidence is extracted from the seized digital devices at the forensic laboratory (i.e., static acquisition). At the forensics laboratory, digital evidence should be acquired in a manner that preserves the integrity of the evidence (i.e., ensuring that the data is unaltered); that is, in a forensically sound manner. To achieve this, the tools and techniques used to acquire digital evidence must prevent alterations to the data or when this is not possible, at the very least minimize them. The seized digital devices are considered as the primary source of evidence. The digital forensics analyst does not acquire data from the primary source. Instead, a duplicate is made of the contents of that device and the analyst works on the copy. This duplicate copy of the content of the digital device (imaging) is created before a static acquisition is conducted to maintain the integrity of digital evidence. To verify whether the duplicate is an exact copy of the original, a cryptographic hash value is calculated for the original and duplicate using mathematical computations; if they match, the copy's contents are a mirror image (i.e., duplicate) of the original content. A write blocker, which is designed to prevent the alteration of data during the copying process, should be used before extraction whenever possible in order to prevent the modification of data during the copying process.

There are two types of extraction performed: physical and logical. Physical extraction involves the search for and acquisition of evidence from the location within a digital device where the evidence resides, such as the hard drive of a computer. A physical extraction may be conducted using keyword searches (based on terms provided by the investigator), filecarving (i.e., search "based on the header, footer, and other identifiers"), and by examining unallocated space (i.e., "space available on a system because it was never used or because the information in it was deleted"; and partitions, which separates segments of the hard drive from each other. Logical extraction involves the search for and acquisition of evidence from the location it "resides relative to the file system of a computer operating system, which is used to keep track of the names and locations of files that are stored on a storage medium such as a hard disk". The type of logical extraction conducted depends on the digital device, file system, applications on the device, and operating system. A logical extraction involves the acquisition of data from active and deleted files, file systems, unallocated and unused space, and compressed, encrypted, and password protected data.

The entire acquisition process should be documented. This documentation should include detailed information about the digital devices from which evidence was extracted, the hardware and software used to acquire the evidence, the manner in which the evidence was acquired (i.e., how it was obtained), when it was obtained, where it was obtained, why it was obtained, what evidence was obtained, and for what reason it was obtained.

Evidence preservation seeks to protect digital evidence from modification. The integrity of digital evidence should be maintained in each phase of the handling of digital evidence (ISO/IEC 27037). First responders, investigators, crime scene technicians, and/or digital forensics experts must demonstrate, wherever possible, that digital evidence was not modified during the identification, collection, and acquisition phase; the ability to do so, of course, depends on the digital device (e.g., computer and mobile phones) and circumstances encountered by them (e.g., need to quickly preserve data). To demonstrate this, a chain of custody must be maintained. The chain of custody is "the process by which investigators preserve the crime (or incident) scene and evidence throughout the life cycle of a case. It includes information about who collected the evidence, where and how the evidence was collected, who took possession of the evidence, and when. In the chain of custody, the names, titles, and contact information of the individuals who identified, collected, and acquired the evidence should be documented, as well as any other individuals the evidence was transferred to, details about the evidence that was transferred, the time and date of transfer, and the purpose of the transfer.

In addition to the handling of digital evidence, the digital forensics process also involves the examination and interpretation of digital evidence (analysis phase), and the communication of the findings of the analysis (presenting or reporting phase). During the analysis phase, digital evidence is extracted from the device, data is analysed, and events are reconstructed. Before the analysis of the digital evidence, the digital forensics analyst in the laboratory must be informed of the objectives of the search, and provided with some background knowledge of the case and any other information that was obtained during the investigation that can assist the forensics analyst in this phase. Various forms of analyses are performed depending on the type of digital evidence sought, such as network, file system, application, video, image, and media analysis (i.e., analysis of data on storage device)

Files are analysed to determine their origin, and when and where the data was created, modified, accessed, downloaded, or uploaded, and the potential connection of these files on storage devices to, for example, remote storage, such as cloud-based storage. The type of digital evidence (e.g., emails, text messages, geo-location, Word processing documents, images, videos, and chat logs) sought depends on the cybercrime case.

Generally, there are four types of analyses that can be performed on computers: time-frame analysis; ownership and possession analysis; application and file analysis; and data hiding analysis. The time-frame analysis seeks to create a timeline or time sequence of actions using time stamps (date and time) that led to an event or to determine the time and date a user performed some action. This analysis is performed to attribute a crime to a perpetrator or at the very least attribute an act that led to a crime to particular individual

Datahiding *analysis* can also be performed. Data hiding analysis searches for hidden data on a system. Criminals use several data-hiding techniques to conceal their illicit activities and identifying information, such as using encryption, password-protecting devices and specific content (e.g., files), changing file extensions, and hiding partitions During the analysis phase, the investigator needs to address the data-hiding techniques that perpetrators could have used to conceal their identities and activities. Hidden data can reveal "knowledge [of a crime], ownership [of content], or intent [to commit a crime.

Ultimately, event reconstruction for the analysis phase uses imperfect knowledge to draw conclusions about a case based on available evidence and analyses of the evidence. For this reason, it is important for cybercrime investigators and digital forensics analysts to recognize these limitations and avoid biased interpretations of the results of these analyses, such as those that result from confirmation bias, where individuals look for and support results that support their working hypothesis and dismiss results that conflict with their working hypothesis

36) Opinion Writing, Preparing Case File or Reporting to Client

The investigator is expected to be proficient in giving the opinion on the case or investigation. The preparation of the case and reporting after the investigations, are key elements to any type of investigations.

Opinion writing – The investigator has to be careful to lay his/her opinion based on the facts of the case and not on any assumption. The opinion of the investigator should not be disclosed to any other official or person.

Preparing Case File – The investigator should document all logs of his activity alongwith his findings and store it on his laptop. The victim's name, contact details with date of commencement of work, and evidential details should be stored at one place pertaining to the case.

Report – The report of the case to the client/victim should primarily contain the factual evidence under 'observations', 'limitations', 'summary' and 'conclusion'. The exhibits so derived should be annexed with the report.

37) Filing a Cyber/Police Complaint

The case will many a times require filing of a cyber/police complaint for seeking/ legalizing the fact finding permissions from the police. The complaint can be filed online in many countries. The procedure of filing may vary from country to country.

In India, the online cyber complaint can be filed on the national portal www.cybercrime.gov.in.

The complaint should necessarily have details of the victim filing the complaint and the sequence of events leading to the fraud or harassment. In case of financial frauds, the screenshots of the SMS, stamped bank statement indicating the transactions are important. For non financial cyber crimes, the screenshots of the conversations/email should be part of the complaint. The contact details of the accused/fraudster and the bank where the money has been transferred are also to be highlighted.

38) Evidence Act Compliance

Depending on the country where the case is being investigated, the evidence act for production of digital evidence (messages, audio, video, etc) in the court of law, the conversation should be digitised before producing in the court of law. In India, 65B of Indian Evidence Act is required to be submitted.

The certificate of 65 B should highlight the following:

a) Description of the manner in which the electronic record was produced.

b) Furnishing of the particulars of the device involved in the production of that record.

c) Dealing with the applicable conditions mentioned under Section 65 B(2) of the Evidence Act.

d) To be signed by a person occupying a responsible official position in relation to the operation of the relevant device.

The person giving the certificate only needs to state in the certificate that the same is to the best of his knowledge and belief.

While preparing the document, following should be kept in mind:

a) The document should be page numbered.

b) The files on which the 65 B is prepared should have the hash value for its integrity.

c) The speakers in the conversation should be identified as per their relation to the subject in question.

39) Investigating GST & PAN details

Most small and medium enterprises do not want to opt for a GSTIN to avoid the compliance cost that comes with it. However, it is very difficult for businesses to operate without a GST number as nobody wants to deal with an unregistered dealer. This ultimately leads to fake GSTINs being printed on an invoice by such dealers.

GST offers various benefits to businesses and a very important benefit is input tax credit. However, for a business to smoothly avail input tax credit, just being compliant is not enough. It also needs to ensure that its business partners i.e. vendors/suppliers are also GST compliant. If they are not registered under GST and use fake GSTIN on their invoices, your business can face problems while filing GST returns and it will not be able to claim input tax credit. Therefore, it is important for you to verify the GSTIN of all your vendors/suppliers.

Format of GST Number

It's an important point to know that GSTIN is of 15 characters which is a combination of numbers and characters. These 15 digits are broken into 5 parts as follows:

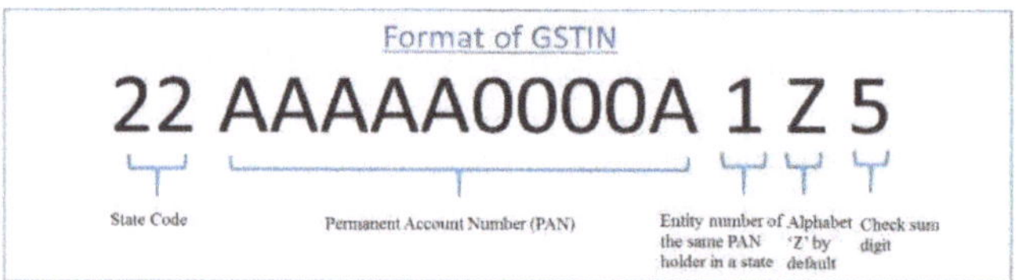

- First 2 digits are state code where the business is registered
- Next 10 digits are PAN number of the business
- The 13th digit is registration number of that store or business with same PAN number
- The 14th digit is Z by default for right now

- The last i.e. 15th digit is a checksum digit code. It may be an alphabet or a number

How to Verify GST Number using GSTN Portal?

Verifying GST Identification Number online is a **very simple** procedure. First, you need to **check the GST Identification Number on the receipt**. It's 100% mandatory to mention GST number on the invoice or bill. If someone is charging GST, without mentioning the GSTIN, then it's illegal. Earlier it was service tax registration number / VAT TIN number, now its GSTIN which must be mandatorily put on the invoice.

Detailed Steps to Check the Validity of GSTIN

- Visit the GST Portal @ **https://www.gst.gov.in**
- Click on "Search Taxpayer" on the menu bar

- Enter GSTIN in search box

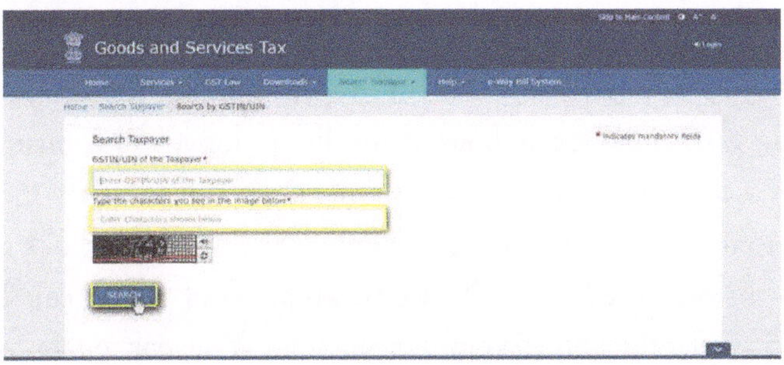

- If the GSTIN is correct you will be able to see the information of the dealer

a) Legal name of business

b) GSTIN / UIN Status

c) Date of registration

d) Constitution of business – company, sole-proprietor or partnership

e) Taxpayer type – regular taxpayer or composition dealer or SEZ unit

- If the GSTIN is incorrect, an error message will be displayed. In this case, you will have to contact your vendor and get the correct GSTIN.

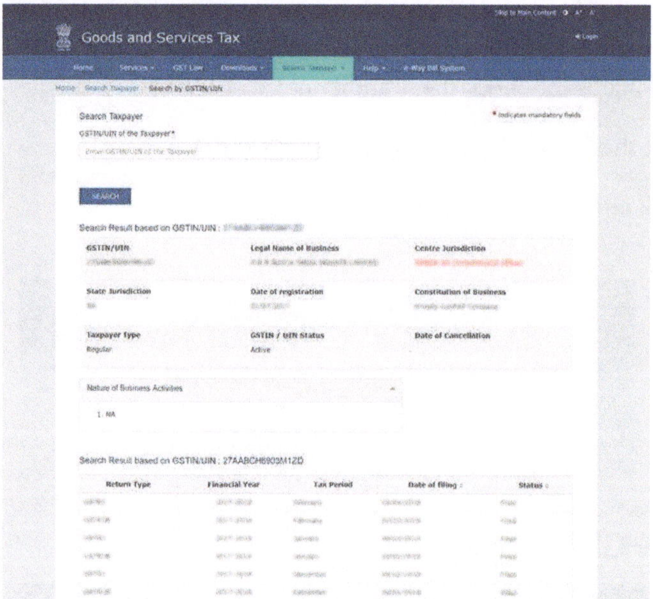

Although you can verify GSTIN of any person on the GST common portal, the task could be tedious if the list is long. As a business, you may have a long list of vendors and you may want to verify their GST numbers to avoid any trouble while filing returns. H&R Block gives you access to an advanced GSTIN Verification Tool which can help you verify GST Identification Numbers in bulk. You can either verify the numbers yourself or share the complete list with us and we will do it for you.

Ways in which GSTIN is Misused

Some businesses still don't have the registration number confirmed, but they have the provisional GSTIN with them, so you can also check the provisional GSTIN online and verify them.

Some shopkeepers and business owners are playing the trick of "I have already applied for GSTIN, Its not yet approved?" This is to give a feeling to customer that they are rightfully charging GST. But this is again a fraud. When they apply for GSTIN, they get a **provisional GSTIN** anyways and they need to either put a GSTIN or provisional GSTIN on the invoice/bill.

Consequences of using a Fake GSTIN

Offences

The offences relevant to fake GSTIN are as follows:

- Making a supply without invoice or with false/ incorrect invoice
- Failure to register despite being liable to be registered
- Issuing invoice or document using GSTIN of another person

Penalties

For all the three cases above the highest penalty leviable shall be 100% of the tax evaded or Rs 10,000 whichever is higher? In a case where any person aids in committing these offences the penalty may extend up to Rs 25,000.

Prosecution

Tax amount evaded	Imprisonment
100 to 200 Lakhs	Up to 1 year and fine

200 to 500 Lakhs	Up to 3 years and fine
Above 500 Lakhs	Up to 5 years and fine

Where and How to Complain about Fake GSTIN?

GST department has dedicated the helplines for you to complain or ask any queries regarding GST. Here are the emails and phone numbers:

- GST Complaint mail id: https://selfservice.gstsystem.in/ or helpdesk@gst.gov.in
- GST Helpline Number: 011-23370115 or 0124-4688999 or 0120-4888999

PAN CARD:

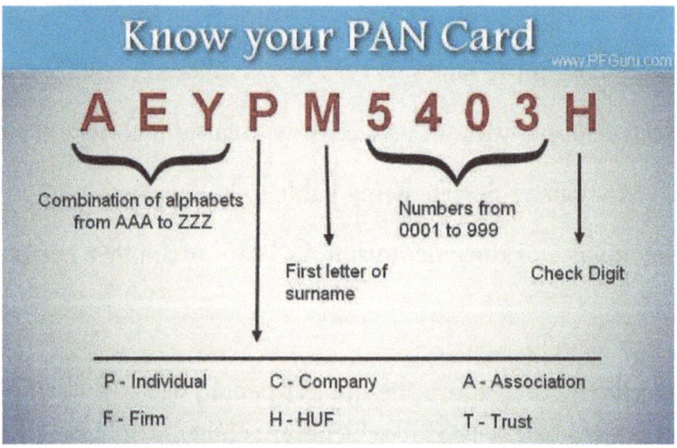

40) Research Tools & Resources

Some utility tools offered by Cyber Crime Helpline LLP, recommended for the Private Investigator are as under:

a) Windows Snap Forensics Tool

b) Windows TOR & VPN Investigative Tool

c) Stealth Password Extractor Tool

d) Hide and Unhide Folders' Tool

41) Bugging Devices

Phone Taps and Phone Bugs

Two terms that are often interchanged but in fact refer to two separate types of attack are Bug and Tap. The differences are:

Tap or Wiretap

This is a device placed on the telephone system and is designed to intercept telephone conversations, i.e. if no call is in place then the tap is inactive.

Bug

A bug is used to listen to room conversation but may use the telephone or line as a facilitator of this. This type of attack means that all conversation in the area is susceptible to being overheard by the attacker and not just telephone calls.

Bugging and Listening devices are in demand in most of the cases pertaining to information gathering. The bugging device types are as under:

GSM Bugs

Perhaps the prolific listening device today, GSM bugs operate in exactly the same way as a mobile phone and a perpetrator can in effect, dial in and silently listen to a conversation from anywhere in the world!

A GSM bug can be a small black box that can be discreetly hidden in a room or it can be a purpose built device such as a mains adaptor, a power strip adaptor, a PC mouse or a phone charger for example. These are everyday objects that one would expect to find in an office, for example, but which could harbour a dangerous secret!

Miniature Voice Recorders

Readily available from online stores, miniature recording devices such as Edic-mini recording devices and those disguised as USB drives or credit cards are discreet audio recording devices designed to be easily hidden or pass undetected by the unwary target. Their use is limited by their battery life and storage, but in many situations they can be just the weapon an infiltrator needs while being affordable and delivering high quality audio.

Mobile Phones as Bugs

Mobile phones themselves can be used as bugging devices. They can be programmed not to vibrate, ring or show any outward signs that they are being called. They then auto-answer and the caller can listen in to conversation within the room.

This type of attack can either be done on a target phone which the perpetrator would then leave somewhere in the vicinity of the conversation they are targeting or it could be done illicitly by installing necessary software onto the target phone. The phone can then be controlled by the hacker who can remotely switch it on and listen from any other mobile phone anywhere in world.

Even when a GSM function is disabled on a Smartphone, the in-built camera can still be used as an eavesdropping device. Smartphones can be used to record video and take photos, stealing product information prototypes etc.

Radio Frequency (RF) Transmitters

A Radio Frequency (RF) bug involves the placing of a radio transmitter in a room and listening within range using a receiver. RF bugs can be incredibly small and can be concealed in just about anything including skirting boards, picture frames, plugs etc. Relatively inexpensive and easy to use, you need a receiver to listen to them.

Radio frequencies are given off by nearly all spying devices, and these radio frequencies can be detected with specialist equipment as used by TSCM engineers. Different types of bugs give off a large range of frequencies and specialist equipment is required to check the entire RF spectrum. Basic RF detectors, that can be purchased relatively cheaply, will only be able to detect limited frequencies and may give a false sense of security, and so its always best to engage the services of a professional service provider.

Optical Devices

Optical devices convert audio signals into transmitted light pulses which are then converted back to audio signals by a receiver. One example of this is the laser attack whereby a laser beam is projected onto a surface, such as a window, and the vibrations detected are converted into audio signals. Laser attacks are difficult and expensive to conduct.

42) De-bugging Devices

De-bugging is a process to detect bugging devices. There are devices to scan for detection of the bugging devices. It is a process in which detection and identification of data transmissions via Wi-Fi, Bluetooth and cellular breaches occur. Debugging is done by deployment of visual and physical search techniques to check the infrastructure to ensure that all potential hiding places, including cables, computers, switches, routers and power sources, etc are scanned.

Types of Devices:

a) RF Detectors – Commercial bugs usually fall in the 10 MHz to 8 MHz range, but some sweeping devices look at 10 hertz all the way to 24 GHz. The RF detectors can detect the radio frequency emitting from the cameras/stealth cameras.

b) Electromagnetic Detectors – For all other types of hidden devices, electromagnetic detectors are used. These are also used to scan for weapons and metallic devices and equipment.

43) Wi-Fi exploitation

Wi-Fi exploitation can lead to information leak. A hacker follows the methodology to penetrate into a corporate or domestic network with default and easy to compromise the corporate network. Following advice in such cases is relevant:-

a) Following advisory is being issued as guidelines to maintain the information security of the office:

i) During the meetings, it is advised to either switch off the mobiles of all the attendees or alternatively, during the meetings, the attendees should keep their mobiles on tables away from the meeting place.

ii) Switch off the router/s wifi accesses

iii) Do not insert any employee/outsiders' pendrive on your laptop/s or PCs without sanitization in a linux machine.

iv) Do not click on any link or photograph/s of any users' pendrive.

v) Have a metallic detector for physical security before entering your meeting area.

vi) Watch out for recording devices like spy pens/recorders in their pockets if visible.

b)Following steps should be taken for enforcing the wifi information security:

i) Seek the ip gateway of the router, user id and password. Default password should be changed. The wifi security should be selected for the most secure mode.

ii) The BSSID should be used to mac filtering for fixed users only and should be monitored by the IT department of the Company. Any addition or removal should be only by the IT staff.

c)The email security will need to be implemented as under:

i)Go to the gmail>>settings tab>>see all settings>>Forwarding and POP/IMAP >>Disable POP and IMAP and remove forwarding email if any

ii) For corporate email>>Go to the control panel of the weblogin>>Check to ascertain if the email has a forwarding email listed here.

PART 4

The Launching Zone

#Fifteen

Ethics and Privacy

Technology is a double-edged sword. Its growth has benefited society in multiple ways, but it has also opened new avenues for bad ethical behaviour, especially the misuse of information. Because personal and business information can be attained, stored, and reproduced so quickly and easily, the danger that it may fall into the wrong hands is greater than ever. Many safeguards have been put in place to protect the public, but those implementing these safeguards are invariably behind the curve due to the proliferation of new technology. Therefore, an individual is on her own and must protect her information. As an investigator, one must safeguard the information of her clients.

1) Ethics and Technology

Cell phones are convenient and provide a feeling of safety. Users typically feel strange without one. Yet these conveniences have become one of the greatest risks to identity and information theft in recent years. One reason is that people using cell phones are everywhere. It's so much so that they've become almost invisible. No one pays attention to anyone taking out a phone (kind of like that car alarm that's barely noticed as it blares away down the street). However, a person with a cell phone could snap pictures of your credit card, driver's license, or personal checks. Even clerks have been known to do this. Because you wouldn't do this, don't be naïve about the number of people who will.

Additionally, you must make sure you safeguard your clients' information just as carefully as you do your own. The following recommended actions will help you accomplish this:

Inventory personal and sensitive client/employee information and its location.

- Determine how this information puts you or your clients at risk---for example, who has access to information and what checks and balances are in place. If the safeguards are insufficient, strengthen them.
- Lock personal and business data away from other files.
- Limit keys to this locked room or cabinet and keep track of who has them.
- Train employees to never let sensitive info out of their sight----not even for short breaks. It only takes a moment to steal information.
- Never leave mail in the box, locked or unlocked, overnight.
- Shred credit card offers and anything that may contain personal information.
- Keep sensitive client information only so long as you have a legitimate business reason for using it.
- If you must use this information, develop a written record retention policy that justifies keeping sensitive client and employee information. Record why you keep it, how long you'll keep it, and when and how you'll dispose of it.
- Receipts must include only the last five numbers of a credit card, not the entire number.

One strategy is to invest in a hidden camera system to help with employee and customer/client accountability. Employees should be trained to handle client/customer information as if it were their own. Many times, data goes missing due to carelessness; employee education can reduce these errors.

Hidden cameras may disclose employee ineptitude, noncompliance with training, or even duplicitous or illegal acts. If you're being watched, have them sign an agreement upon being hired which informs them that they may be subject to periodic surveillance of their duties. Be sure to include that this is for the purpose of quality control and any needed retraining.

Then follow through and either record them periodically (cameras can be rented for this purpose) or have a covert system installed.

2) Ethics and Obtaining Evidence

Illegally obtained information is of no more use to the Private Investigator than it is to the law enforcement investigator. However, a fine line exists between legal and illegal and between good and bad ethics. In those rare moments when noting but conscience is available to guide the investigator, the investigator should always lean toward the legal and choose the good. By doing so, the investigator not only protects the evidence and the client, he/she protects himself/herself as well.

You'll need to cultivate contacts with all types of people. People possess information you need, and getting it can be dicey. You must make choices as to the line you can walk without crossing it. Some investigators have cultivated relationships with people who have access to prohibited information. For instance, they have bribed phone company employees to get unlisted phone numbers and protected addresses; in some cases, unethical investigators have persuaded phone company employees to let them listen in on private conversations.

3) Consent

Employers and investigators who perform background checks must notify the applicant of their intent to run the check and must obtain a signed consent to do so as recommended by the Fair Credit Reporting Act (FCRA). In fact, higher-level information services require that you state the reason for running at least some parts of the background checks. You can run subject into such as alias, social security number verifier, addresses and phone numbers, court and business records, licenses other than driver's license, and surrounding neighbourhood facilities, all without stating your purpose. The moment you request driver's license information, licensed drivers at residence, and vehicles registered at address, one must name the purpose from this list:

- To protect against or prevent actual or potential fraud, unauthorized transactions, claims or other liability
- For required institutional risk control or resolving consuming disputes or inquiries
- Due to holding a legal beneficial interest relating to the subject
- To effect, administer, or enforce a transaction to underwrite insurance at the consumer's insurance's request, for reinsurance purposes, or for (relating to consumer's insurance) reporting, investigating, fraud prevention, premium payment processing, benefit administration, or research projects

A consent, or release form, is standard in most companies, but if you perform searches for employers you must obtain a copy of the consent as well. Also, the consent must be worded to include permission for you to perform the search. If it doesn't include you by name, it should indicate permission for an agent of the company to do the background check.

4) Choosing an Information Database

The fact is that there are few fully functional systems that can deliver what is advertised, with permissions/authorisations to use them. Working on their rigorous requirements may take time, effort, and necessary qualifications, time and effort that many are unwilling to spend with authorisations and capability that is generally not available. Another not-so-widely-known fact is that not only do this information may not be sufficient to do proper due diligence on perspective employees.

5) Due Diligence

Due diligence is the **process** of examining the details of a transaction, association, agreement between two or more organisations/agencies to make sure it's legal, and to fully apprise the respective parties of as many facts in the deal as possible. When the deal satisfies both aspects of **due diligence**, the two parties can finalize and correctly price the transaction.

The different types of due diligence

- Buying a company due diligence. ...
- M&A due diligence. ...
- Financial due diligence. ...
- Customer due diligence. ...
- Commercial due diligence. ...
- Vendor due diligence. ...
- Third Party due diligence. ...
- The richest source of company information.

6) Database Services

The best database services receive most of their information from state and federal records, not from middlemen. Receiving information from databases whose information has come from other databases increases the possibility of human input error. The better services also update records every few days; some do it daily. Information remains the same.

It is also possible to have an insurance policy if available, for those who provide background and pre-employment searches. Though rare, even when using a capable information database, errors over which you have no control cannot be ruled out.One is expected to avoid any risk losing everything in the absence of this insurance.

In light of these things, it's easier to understand how systems that are hooked into fewer national law enforcement databases and connected more distantly than NCIC are also fallible. This means that event even the best service provider is subject to errors now and then. When running reports for your clients, you should counsel them about this possibility in order to present a realistic picture of the information business. While it may be rare that the information returned from your service provider contains errors or omissions, your client should be prepared for this possibility. Otherwise, if it happens, he can feel that you've been negligent or worse, that you've been intentionally dishonest.

#Sixteen

Working with Law

1) Arrest Law

Police powers come equipped with the authority to arrest in clearly defined situations. As a private investigator, you aren't given this broad authority. Your authority to arrest is the same as any other citizen's, the parameters of which are listed later in this section. Understanding this is especially important for PIs working with attorneys and police agencies.

2) Police Powers of Arrest and Detention

The police has all powers for arrest and detention of the subject. If a FIR (First Information Report) is lodged, police can arrest, however, detention could be a prelude before filing a FIR. The difference between arrest and detention can be confusing, there is however a definite line between the two. Many standards of proof have been set in place to justify an officer's arrest and detention of citizens while protecting the rights of those citizens. However, only an overview of the most common standards will be discussed here. The main difference between detention and arrest is whether a person is charged with a crime or not. In case of a person being detained, he is not formally accused of committing a crime but is simply restricted and kept in police custody on a reasonable suspicion or clarification. Thus, detention may be seen as a lesser form of arrest. Requirement of a lawyer for intervention may be required for bailing out the person in such custody.

Several situations exist where an officer can arrest without a warrant. Some of these are:

- An offense, misdemeanour, or offence committed within the presence or view of the officer

- When a person believed to be creditable informs the officer of a felony and there's no time to obtain a warrant
- To prevent theft, a breach of the peace, or injury
- Upon the order of a magistrate before whom a felony or breach of the peace has occurred
- Officer hears an admission of guilt or a statement made by witness as the crime is committed or immediately after (sometimes ruled an excited utterance)
- Reasonable suspicion: officer believes suspect has done something but isn't necessarily sure what it is; officer can detain briefly and frisk (not a full search, but a pat down for weapons to protect himself); evidence found in a frisk isn't admissible, but under certain circumstances a frisk can turn into a legal search

Probable cause defined as facts or evidence that would lead a reasonable or cautious person to believe a crime has been, is being, or will be committed; the difference between this and reasonable suspicion is that the officer usually knows what crime he suspects the subject of committing and has evidence to support this. An officer could claim probable cause when he stops a vehicle and views, in plain sight, contraband such as drugs, burglary tools, or the like. Probable cause is strengthened is strengthened in the case of burglary tools if burglaries have taken place in the area and/or the suspect or her vehicle fits the description given by witnesses.

3) The Law of Evidence

The laws of evidence are lengthy and complicated, and many books have been written on the subject. Therefore, while this overview is thorough enough for most readers, it's also intended as a guide for further research for those who want more.

Types of Evidence

Should you continue your study, you'll find that authors differ in their manner of classifying evidence. Some write that there are three types, while others list four, and still others break evidence down into many more categories. For the purpose of this book, there are four kinds of evidence; testimonial, real, documentary, and demonstrative evidence. Other types referred to in investigations and in court are usually subtypes of these many of them often overlap:

- Testimonial evidence (verbal or written) can be statements, interviews, depositions, and confessions.

- Real evidence is anything whose materiality and relevance are obvious, and which is directly involved in a case. Also called physical evidence, it can be a weapon, a wrecked automobile, a bloody shirt, or forensic and trace evidence such as DNA, hairs, and fibres.

- Demonstrative evidence is anything that is the representation of an object. It can be photos; x-rays; audio and video recordings; illustrations; maps; computer simulation, animation, and reconstruction; models; and more.

- Documentary evidence is anything in the form of documents that is presented in order to examine its contents. It can be records (written, printed, on film, microfiche, etc.) such as wills, contracts, letters, invoices, and printed e-mails. It is subject to authentication, usually by testimony. Documents presented for a different purpose, such as proving that they were handled and contain prints from a victim or suspect, are real evidence, but they may be documentary as well if the contents are relevant.

There are rules of evidence which addresses evidence as it relates to that which can be testified to. The rules, however, apply to all evidence.

Some of these rules apply to every type of evidence, some only apply to one, and some apply to several types.

4) Testifying in Court

Many cases never go to court, some are commissioned by clients who merely want information, some are settled between the client and the target, and others are settled by attorneys. How many of your cases will end up in court is also dependant on the type of investigations you work. When the courtroom is the last step in working a case, it's an extremely important one. Therefore, it's vital that you understand basic courtroom procedures and legalities.

5) Accepting a Court Order

If the client has attorney, he/she doesn't need to send you a court order for your testimony. However, if the other side wants to question you, either on the stand or in a deposition, they must send one. Be aware that your client cannot prevent you from accepting a court order even though you work for her.

Some firms, and even individual clients, will send the investigator out of town to avoid his acceptance of a court order. This is not only unprofessional, it is a bold attempt to bypass the judicial system, and it will be obvious to the court. A court order is a legal order for you to appear in court and it's an order, not a request. If you don't appear, you can be held in disrespect.

Be professional. Don't hide. Accepting the court order shows respect for the person serving it and for the judicial system. You never know when you may meet her or others associated with the case. One day, you may need her help or she may need a Private Investigator. Never burn your bridges with anyone.

An investigator entitled to payment for her time in court. Bill your client. Even when you are called by opposing counsel, your testimony is beneficial to your client's case and plays a vital part in the investigation. Include charges for court testimony in the client agreement. Because you're unavailable to work other cases, you're entitled to payment for time spent waiting to testify, not only for time spent on the stand. Travel expenses are also billable, should they apply.

You may be called for a deposition. These are usually held in the attorney's office or that of the court reporter. A deposition is a statement made under oath and in front of witnesses (attorneys for both sides are usually present) that becomes an official record that can be used in court. It's usually written and signed by the person being deposed as well as the witnesses. It is often videoed as well.

Because depositions are quite costly, the PI is important in this process. In addition to being interviewed, the PI is also often used to interview multiple witnesses and return reports to the attorney, who uses the information to choose the witnesses she wants to depose. In this way, she won't have to pay of depositions that won't be useful to the case. Since payment for the PI's time is usually much less than the cost of depositions, total expenses can be reduced.

6) Behaviour and Dress

Proper courtroom attire is stylish, but conservative. If you appear in outdated styles, some jury members, especially younger ones, may view you as a throwback from another generation. Unfortunately, this could affect the way your testimony is evaluated. Stylish doesn't mean faddish; avoid clothing that may be in one year and out the next or styles that can be acceptable in another situation but are too casual, radical, distracting, or revealing for the formality of a courtroom. Classic colours and styles with updated cuts and fabrics are the best choices, and they stamp you as someone with dignity and taste. Attire should enhance your professional image without drawing attention to what you wear.

Men are required to wear suits or jackets and ties. Women must wear either dresses or professional suits with skirts or pants.

In jurisdictions without such rules, the Private Investigator should investigate and follow the accepted dress and behaviour of attorneys who regularly appear in court. Further rules to follow are:

- Always be on time. This cannot be overstated.
- You will be searched long before you get inside the courtroom, so don't bring weapons; they're not allowed in the building.
- The removal of hats is considered respectful, and often required, before entering a courtroom. The exception is religious attire.
- Refrain from doing anything to distract the process, such as coming in and out excessively, talking loudly, tapping your foot, or moving around in your seat too much.
- Don't eat, drink, or chew gum.
- Don't slouch, look disinterested, or roll your eyes when you disagree with a statement.
- Keep your hands away from your face and resting calmly in your lap.
- Look directly at your questioner during questioning and when answering him.
- Turn off all cell phones or paging devices; most jurisdictions also ban the use of laptops or the reading of newspapers and books in court.
- Don't bring recording devices into the courtroom without prior approval of the judge.

If you haven't testified in court or been chosen for jury duty, you may not understand the importance of these rules. If not, please understand one thing: when you are in court, you can likely to be watched and evaluated, whether you testify or not. If you testify, you'll be investigated.

7) Difference between Civil and Criminal Trials

Civil trials are concerned with resolution of claims by individuals or groups against other individuals or groups. In reaching a decision, the burden of proof is governed by "a preponderance (or weight) of evidence." Criminal trials deal with prosecuting those accused of violating criminal law. The burden of proof (for proving guilt) in a criminal trial is "beyond a reasonable doubt," a stricter standard.

8) Court Procedures

The court has the power to make decisions and also enforce the law, solve disputes. Judiciary system consists of Judges and other magistrates, they form the bench or the core of the judiciary system. The Judicial System of India consists of Supreme Court, High Court, District Court or Subordinate Court.

The first attorney (usually the defense) will begin by questioning a witness during what's called direct examination. Cross-examination follows, where opposing counsel either questions the witness or passes. Only subjects brought up or introduced during direct examination can be questioned in cross-examination, unless the judge chooses to allow it. In re-direct, the original attorney can again question a witness to clear up anything that's unclear or has been introduced or distorted by cross-examination. This can be followed by re-cross. During questioning, either side can object to specific questions. Responses to objections are as follows:

- **Judge can overrule:** witness is permitted to provide the answer
- **Judge can sustain:** question must be asked again in a different way
- **Judge can ask for further information** so she can decide how to rule

When an objection is made, it's important that you stop talking immediately and wait for the judge's response. One a ruling is made, you'll know what to do. If the question is sustained, you must answer. If it's overruled, you must wait for the next question. The most common objections you'll hear in court follow:

- **Leading the witness.** A leading question suggests the answer: Didn't you see the subject driving erratically? Is non-leading. Did you see the subject driving? In your opinion, how was she handling the vehicle?
- **Hearsay.** A statement made by someone other than the testifying witness. There are many exceptions, some of which will be discussed later.
- **Relevancy.** Questions and statements may be challenged if they do not directly relate to the case.

Leading questions are allowed on cross-examination when the attorney is questioning an unfriendly witness. They aren't allowed during direct questioning, when the attorney for whom you work questions you, because leading questions suggest the answer for the witness to supply. However, when your attorney asks a leading question, knowing it'll probably b objected to and overruled by the judge, it's a clue as to where he wants you to go with your answer.

Hearsay evidence may be accepted under several conditions:

- **Dying declaration.** Although it is hearsay because the person declaring isn't in court, a person who heard a dying person's statement may repeat that statement because of the general belief that someone aware of dying doesn't have any reason to lie. For example, "I heard her say, 'John stabbed me.'"
- **Excited utterance.** It is still hearsay if the person who uttered the statement isn't in court, but this is admissible testimony because in the heat of an exciting incident, a witness may blurt out something ran over that little boy."
- **Admission against interest.** A witness can testify that she heard a party in a lawsuit make a statement that runs counter to the party's

case. For example, a witness can testify she heard the suspect admit he committed the crime for which he is on trial.

- **Business records.** These must be introduced by a qualified witness who can identify them and testify how they were recorded.
- **Official government records** that have been properly maintained.
- **Notes.** These must be made close to the time of an event and can be used during testimony to refresh the memory of a witness.
- **Judgments in other cases.**
- **Statement explaining a person's future plans.** For example, "I' m going to choke the life out of her and keep her from hurting anyone again." The person who heard this can testify to what was said.

9) Circumstantial Evidence

This type of evidence doesn't prove the existence of a fact at least not directly. It does, however, provide logical suspicion that the fact exists, but reasoning is required to prove its existence. The general belief is that circumstantial evidence is weak, but often this type of evidence proves a case, as physical evidence isn't always available.

The compilation of inferential evidence can lead to the belief that no other conclusion is possible. For example, the defendant may have been seen in the area around the time of the murder. He may have been heard threatening the deceased and may have owned the weapon that killed her. He may also have hurt the deceased in the past. His prints may even be in the house, but they are considered circumstantial if he has been in the house before. All of these things are circumstantial, but together they begin to point to a strong conclusion. If you have enough of them, they make a case.

10) Audio-visual Media

Photographs or video recordings of evidence are important to your case. In order to be admissible, someone must testify that they reasonably represent the thing or person that was photographed or filmed. The person giving testimony concerning the item either must have taken it herself or been present when it was taken, so she can verify that the film or photograph accurately represents what it is purported to represent.

Charts, modes, and maps, sometimes called demonstrative evidence, are not evidence in and of themselves; they must be authenticated, usually with the testimony of the person using these objects. They are used in court to make a point or to demonstrate a fact, and marks made on these items may be used to prove a fact. If so, they may be admitted into evidence. Again, admissibility is at the discretion of the judge.

11) Video Surveillance Law

Thirteen states prohibit camera installation in private areas; defined as areas in which people have an expectation of privacy. This expectation is a legal one. The following places are protected in many states:

- Private homes
- Public and private bathrooms
- Public changing rooms
- Hotel rooms
- Rental homes and apartments
- Bedrooms

There are some exceptions. For example, you have an expectation of privacy in your own home, but if you leave your drapes open, you shouldn't expect that no one will look in. you have no legal expectation in this case. Neither do you have an expectation that you won't be filmed---if the person filming is standing where it's legal for her to stand, such as on the street or sidewalk. If she's on your property, she's trespassing and the expectation stands.

12) Cross Examination Response

Newly joined Private Investigators are usually nervous about being cross-examined by opposing counsel. If you are, you're in good company then almost everyone is nervous about this, at least a little. The more you testify, however, the less you'll dread cross-examination. When you understand that it's counsel's job to rattle you and there's nothing personal about it, you'll also understand that it's your job to stay cool.

Speak Clearly and Confidently

Practice speaking in a clear and modulated voice. Don't hesitate long I answering opposing counsel's questions. She can use this hesitation to insinuate that you're manufacturing an answer in the best interest of your client instead of answering truthfully. However, don't speak so quickly that it appears you're not thinking seriously about your answer. Speaking too quickly can also prevent your attorney from having time to object before the answer leaves your mouth. Never, never volunteer information. Answer only what you are asked. If your attorney wants to bring out further evidence, he can do so later.

Be cautious of the attorney whose aim is to discredit you and who tries to cause you to react with anger, embarrassment, and/or defensiveness. Provide slow, respectful, deliberated answers to any attacks on your character or capability. Also, be careful of the overly friendly attorney who attempts to catch you off guard with a not-so-friendly question. Remember, it's not personal.

Avoid using profanity, jargon, cop-speak, or slang, unless you're directly quoting someone. The jury has a few minutes to decide what type of person you are and whether they believe you. Don't use offensive language or present an attitude that might alienate some jury members. Be respectful to both parties and address the defendant as Mr., Mrs., or

Ms. Whoever, etcand sarcasm or disapproval when relating the subject's actions is to be avoided.

13) Be Prepared

After receiving a court's order, contact the attorney for whom you're working. She will want to discuss the types of questions you may be asked and prepare you for the more difficult aspects of the case.

Using Your Notes

Before you get on the stand, review all the information you have in your report and notes. You don't have to memorize everything, but refresh your memory as to important times, dates, and incidences. If the case is long or complicated, you're allowed to take your notes to the stand for the purpose of finding and confirming dates, times, or specific details that they may wise be fuzzy in your memory. However, if you do so, know that they may be made available to the other side for inspection, and they could be placed into evidence. At the very least, the portion that is ruled to be related to the case can be entered into evidence. Talk to your attorney first.

The jury members may see you from the moment you leave home. You may be in traffic or on the bus with jurors. You may run into a convenience store or get gas at the same location, or be together in the courthouse or restroom prior to trial. They not know you until you testify, but they'll remember an inappropriate or ugly scene, and they will judge your testimony by your behaviour and attitude.

In civil cases, your notes and reports are subject to discovery anyway. Another point to remember: Accuracy is important in any case, but be aware that when the other side gets your reports and notes, opposing counsel will comb through them booking for mistakes on which to build their case and cause doubt in the minds of the jury members.

Tell the Truth

Always tell the truth. This not only allows you to live a life of integrity, it's a means of keeping you from the attorney's trap. When you're on the witness stand, opposing counsel may attempt to lure you into an argumentative posture by asking unanswerable questions.

Even when you tell the truth, it's the job of opposing counsel to try to confuse you and poke holes in your testimony. By misrepresenting anything, you play into her hands. Lies are difficult to keep straight, especially under the pressure of cross-examination. Tell the truth and you won't have to worry about concocting another lie to cover the one before it.

You get the picture. The opposing counsel is trying to place doubt in the mind of the jury members; doubt that you saw what you saw or worse, doubt that you haven't done job properly. The only defense is to answer truthfully and without emotion. Being truthful will enhance your credibility and could even cause counsel to appear to be repeatedly ask you. Most jury members don't like that.

#Seventeen

Complaint and Investigations

1) Interviewing Children

If a child returns with stories that seem made up or imaginary, be open to the fact that they may be true. This is especially hard for the child's parent or caretaker. No spouse wants to think that they've married someone who could abuse or allow someone else to abuse a child. Some people are so pained by the thought of their child being hurt they can't bear to believe it happened. Some want to believe that the child misinterpreted an innocent action. Others are remiss what's right in front of them. Still others believe that children are fanciful and imaginative, and that their testimony is not as trustworthy as that of adults. The little-known truth is that children's testimony, if not contaminated or tampered with, is quite reliable. Some experts believe it's more reliable than any adult testimony. Children stay in the moment more than adults. They're not thinking about what to fix supper or how to pay the phone bill. They're present and aware most of the time. See Chapter 19 for more information on interviewing witnesses, including child witnesses.

Clients often place hidden cameras or voice recorders in the lining of their child's bag or in a favourite doll or stuffed animal in order to discover what happens on visiting day with a parent or grandparent. This can backfire. If the materials are discovered, your case may be over. The target will always be suspicious that she's being watched and alter her behaviour accordingly; at least until the settlement is over.

Investigators should survey the target and record anything questionable about his treatment of the child. In some cases, the client should also buy or rent a camera. If the child persists in her stories, the client may need to record her spontaneous remarks, but they must be unsolicited and made with the child unaware of the recording. Have the client set up a camera and discreetly turn it on when the child begins to speak of suspicious incidents. The child can be asked to repeat what's been said but cannot be prompted or asked leading questions. Leading questions are those that direct someone to answer in a predetermined manner.

Children have returned from a visit with a parent, grandparent, relative, or babysitter with stories of being shut up in locked rooms or closets, of being hungry or left alone for hours, and of physical abuse. Parents would much rather believe that stories such as these are tall tales or dreams, but the horrible truth is that these things and worse actually happen. Counsel your client to never accuse her child of lying when he tells stories such as these. Help your client find the truth before making judgments.

2) Registering Children for Future Identification

Registering children is a controversial issue. Some are concerned about privacy issues. Others see the collection of this information as a necessary protection from real evils.

Fingerprinting Children

In your investigation, you must discover if the parents have had the child fingerprinted. This is especially important in cases of very young children whose appearance will change, sometimes drastically, as they grow. Note that fingerprinting isn't important only for finding and identifying a body, but live child have been identified through stored fingerprints.

Is fingerprinting children an overreaction to the possibility of their abduction?

Most experts recognize that the small effort involved in fingerprinting a child may provide huge gains if the unthinkable happens and the child goes missing.

If the child was abducted before she could talk, fingerprints are vital to identifying her later, especially if she does not have any birthmarks or unique identifiers. Even older children may be unable to aid in their own identification, having little memory of their life prior to being abducted. Not every parent has a child fingerprinted, however. Some are a bit superstitious, saying they don't want to tempt fate. Others don't even like to think about the possibility. Still others have fingerprinting on their list of things to accomplish, but never get around to it.

Having your child's fingerprints on record can be very useful if your child ever goes missing.

There is a very small group that is afraid of fingerprinting children due to privacy concerns. These people fear that the government will gain control of any database, which may fall into the wrong hands and be used against their children in the future. Others feel that the likelihood of their child being abducted is so low that they do not need to have their child fingerprinted.

#Eighteen

Statements and Confessions

Statement: Any written or verbal communication that might be of help to implicate a suspect's involvement in a crime. For example, a witness could give a statement. It is preferable to have some documentary evidence in written form to avoid any likely change from the witness or person giving statement.

Confession: An admission of all material facts that isconsidered necessary to prove each or any part of the offence and any partial admission of one or more of the material facts that assists in proving the guilty.

Confession refers to a voluntary statement made by the person who has been accused of committing a crime. It is a direct acknowledgment of guilt by the accused. On the other hand, admission, while also being a voluntary statement, is merely the acknowledgment that a particular fact is true.

There is always the chance that the accused might have accepted the crime under the force and coercive means used by the police. Hence, there is a rule that confessions made during police custody cannot be used as evidence against the accused

Corpus delicti (Latin: 'body of the crime'; plural: corpora delicti) is a term from Western jurisprudence referring to the principle that a crime must be proved to have occurred before a person can be convicted of committing that crime.

The elements of Corpus delicti:

(1) Actusreus—The guilty act (2) Mensrea—The guilty mind (3) Concurrence—The coexistence of (1) an act in violation of the law and (2) a culpable mental state (4) Causation—The concurrence of mind and act must produce harm.

The 'writ of habeas corpus', often shortened to 'habeas corpus', is the requirement that an arrested person be brought before a judge or court before being detained or imprisoned.

#Nineteen

Business Models

There are many business models from which to choose, but if you're a newbie, it's safest to go with an established type. An overview of the most-used models may help you choose the one that best fits your needs.

1) Types of Companies in India

a) Private Limited Company: -

A private limited company, is a type of privately held small business entity. This type of business entity limits owner liability to their shares, limits the number of shareholders to 50, and restricts shareholders from publicly trading shares, does not invite public to subscribe to its share capital. Must have a minimum paid up capital of Rs. 1 lakh or such a higher amount which may be prescribed from time to time.

b) Public Limited Company: -

A public limited company is a joint-stock company. It is governed under the provisions of the Indian Companies Act, 2013. While there is no limit on the number of members but minimum it should be 7 and it is formed by the association of persons voluntarily with a minimum paid-up capital of 5 lakh rupees.

c) Unlimited Company: -

An unlimited company is a type of private company. It has some features similar to a limited company. However, the shareholders (or members) of this type of company have unlimited liability. This means each member is jointly and severally liable for the debts of the company in the event of its insolvent winding-up. Unlimited Company is a form of business organization under which the liability of all its members is unlimited. The personal assets of the members can be used to settle the debts. It can at any time re-register as a limited company under section 32 of the Companies Act.

d) Sole Proprietorship: -

A sole proprietorship is one of the easiest and simplest form of business entity to register and maintain in India. There is no formal sole proprietorship registration and to start a proprietorship only PAN number for the Proprietor, certain licenses and capital is required. It is a form of business entity where a single individual handles the entire business organization. He is the sole recipient of all profits and bearer of all loses. There is no separate law that governs sole proprietorship.

e) Joint Hindu Family Business: -

In Hindu religion, Joint family business, a particular form of business organization found only in India which is considered as one of the oldest form of business organization in the country wherein the members of a family can only own and manage the business. It refers to the kind of organization in which the business is owned and run by the members of the Hindu Undivided Family(HUF). It is governed by Hindu Law.

f) Partnership: -

Partnership is "the relation between persons who have agreed to share the profits of the business carried on by all or any one of them acting for all". It is governed by the Indian Partnership Act 1932.

g) Cooperatives: -

Co-operatives is a form of voluntary organization, wherein the members work together for the promotion of the interests of its members. There is no restriction to the entry or exit of any member. It is governed by Cooperative Societies Act 1912.

h) Trust Company: -

A trust company is a corporation that acts as a fiduciary, trustee or agent of trusts and agencies. A professional trust company may be independently owned or owned by, for example, a bank or a law firm, and which specializes in being a trustee of various kinds of trusts.

i) Limited Liability Partnership: -

Under LLP (Limited Liability Partnership) the liability of at least one member is unlimited whereas rest all the other members have limited liability, limited to the extent of their contribution in the LLP. Unlike general partnership this kind of partnership does not get terminated by the death or insolvency of the limited partners. It is governed by Limited Liability Partnership Act of 2008.

j) Sole Proprietorship: -

One owner is responsible for the entire operation and for all business debt. He/she takes the risks, and she reaps the benefits. Yet being a sole proprietor doesn't mean that the risks, and she reaps the owner is in business all alone. He/she may employ many people, but hasn't created any formal structure such as a corporation or LLC.

One disadvantage of a sole proprietorship is that personal assets aren't protected from litigation or creditors. Another is that the owner must pay taxes on all profit as income, whether or not she pays herself a salary. For example, when business expenses are deducted from the total business income, whatever remains is assessed as income to the owner. On top of this, the owner is subject to self-employment tax on all income, a tax shared between employee and business under a corporation. A sole proprietor pays her share and the business's share. However, the sole proprietorship is a simple operation with little regulation, so some business owners prefer it to other business models.

2) Pro and Cons of Business Ownership

Owning and operating a business can be lucrative, but it's not for everyone. The numbers of businesses that go under each year attests to this fact. Yet sometimes, everything works together to cause a specific product or service, offered at the right time, in the right place, and in the right manner, to capture public attention and meet public need. This is not accidental, however; it takes a lot of work. Know the risks and benefits before you begin.

3) Aspects of Business Ownership

Some advantages of owning a small business include:

- Flexibility of schedule----though you may work more hours, you decide when
- Freedom to choose jobs you want and refuse ones you don't want
- Freedom to perform your work your way
- Freedom to outsource the boring stuff and concentrate on creative business building
- Opportunity to better meet specialty client needs and requests
- Opportunity for increased earning capacity and decreased tax liability
- Opportunity, using the Internet, to look and perform big without big business costs
- Opportunity to love what you do and do what you love.

Remember that ending up with a successful business entity will depend on how much preparation you're willing to expend at the beginning.

Business Description

In business description it must include the name and particulars of your business: address, phone numbers, Web site, and other relevant information.

Business Location

Describe the potential client and the location that will draw him to your business. Will you seek the high-end client? Attorneys and professionals? If so, take a walk through their offices to get a feel for the atmosphere that says success to them. If you can afford it, create this atmosphere in your office.

Principal Services or Products

Describe the services that you've listed earlier. Be specific. Will you perform the services yourself, or will some require skills you don't possess? Will you purchase special equipment in order to offer these services? If you sell products, describe them, along with any restrictions on their use or special storage and/or display requirements.

4) Market and Competition for Services or Products

Who is your market? Where are they located? Why are they a possible market for your products or services? Consider who your competitors are, how they conduct business, and what their fees are.

Do a little survey to determine the competition's marketing scheme, line of products, services, pricing, and fees. Be careful, however; don't become over excited and openly take notes or ask too many questions. No one likes observing or spying and to speak into a small tape recorder. You need to do this discretely.

5) Available Management and Resource Personnel

Who will work with you and what are their strengths? What are their backgrounds and skills? Profile your accountant, attorney, and any associates or investors. Do the same with consultants, but remember that this plan is for you. Allow it to show you where the holes exist in your management team so they can be filled with competent employees, consultants, or resource personnel.

#Twenty

Setting up Your Private Investigation

Setting up a private investigator business is not difficult at all. One can work independently depending on time and convenience without being answerable to anyone. You would be responsible for your cases and employees growth.

1) Essential Items for a Private Investigator

- ✓ Files/Stationery, Office space with secure storage for client & subject's information, and equipped with a computer, printer, and shredder.
- ✓ Registering with State/Central Govt Authorities
- ✓ Shop Act License/Udyog Aadhar as per requirement
- ✓ Bank Account in the name of business
- ✓ Laptop/PC
- ✓ Acquiring Surveillance Devices
- ✓ Couple of mobile SIMs
- ✓ An up-to-date computer, preferably a laptop
- ✓ A web site/blogs and social media pages
- ✓ Business cards and identity card with wearable badge
- ✓ A reliable vehicle of normal appearance.
- ✓ A video camcorder of low-lux image stabilization, zoom lens with auto control features and foldable but sturdy tripod.
- ✓ A good binocular and/or terrestrial telescope with digital and optical zoom features.

- ✓ Communication equipment, radios, and a good cell phone
- ✓ A wearable or portable covert camera
- ✓ Some specs of different wigs and disguising outfits
- ✓ Cyber/digital toolkit for surveillance, key loggers and digital extraction tools (Optional)

2) Business/Corporate Security and Investigations

Business and corporate security offers a wider variety of opportunities for the PI than any other specialty. These opportunities include worker's compensation, accident and arson investigation, fraud (including medical and corporate fraud), theft of time or products or services, undercover investigation, product liability and wrongful injury investigation, background and pre-employment investigation, document/data analysis and forensic accounting, repossessions and collections, and process service.

3) Disclosure of Recording in Office Spaces

In view of higher sensitivity of business gains, the organisations focus mainly to protect their assets. Whether the business resorts to audio or video camera installation/recording or enforcing any type of surveillance in the office space to nab personnel against theft or monitor their poor work performance. Installation of covert cameras for recording or for live streaming purposes is generally resorted to, by their businesses. The owners may or may not inform their employees of the existence of these cameras. The owners have full rights to record video or audio with it.

Some owners choose to inform employees that there may be cameras watching and listening to them at any time. In this case, it's best to have the employee sign a disclosure confirming that he's been informed of possible surveillance. By disclosing the existence of the cameras, the employer can record audio. Because the cameras are hidden and sometimes remarkably, so the employee will never be sure if he's being monitored, nor will he know the location of monitoring devices. With this strategy, one purpose for installing covert cameras can still be achieved if the employee will refrain from theft of products or services, or his theft will be disclosed. This should also increase employee productivity and quality of client or customer service.

By informing clients that they may be monitored and having them sign that they've been informed, all three problems that plague businesses most-theft of time, products, and services that can be addressed, along with the added bonus of improved customer service.

In regard to telephone monitoring, should the employer want to monitor every employee's interaction with customers as a matter of policy and for training, the law allows the owner to do so. Personal conversation is generally not allowed in the offices and if permitted should not be recorded if the system access is easy. Generally the business owners who monitor don't do so themselves, but since automated systems cannot determine which part of a conversation is about business and which is personal, the cameras record or stream all. If the owner informs the employee or displays that monitoring or surveillance will occur, the recording is considered legal.

4) Medical Fraud

Doctors and other medical service providers are in a position, should they choose, to defraud insurance companies. While most do not, a large and growing number of medical professionals have chosen to make a side business of padding patients' bills. Even otherwise legitimate doctors have been known to do this occasionally in order to meet payroll or cover losses.

Most patients never scrutinize medical bills unless they're ridiculously long or more expensive than expected. Even when patients do study their bills, they're almost impossible to fully understand unless you work in the field. Medical criminals know this and count on it. Some medical service providers have learned to spread their fraudulent charges over a wide range of patens and dates. These professionals have also been known to charge for visits and services for patients who were never seen, keeping the patient from looking to closely into the transaction by having any refund sent to him. Because the patient benefits, many who realize what's going on just let it go. In this way, they're silent accomplices to fraud because they allow it to continue. Because of all these things, it's not unusual for patients to pay fraudulent medical claims for years before the deceit is discovered.

Other physicians insist that a personal injury claim be filed after an accident, even when the patient is uninjured. Another problem is that of suspect attorneys claiming that a client was injured on someone's properly, when no one but witnesses she produces can verify the facts of the injury. These attorneys and cohorts have been known to deliberately stage accidents, destroy property, and fake injuries.

One of the worst problems in this area is accident-chasing attorneys. Since attorneys who appear at accident scenes have long been charged with the unflattering tile of ambulance chasers, many use different tactics. One is to send cappers or runners to scenes in the guise of caring witnesses. Cappers direct injures parties to their bosses, unscrupulous doctors and/or attorneys.

Then there are the organized criminal enterprises that engage in fraudulent billing of insurance companies. Called mill, these enterprises bilk insurance companies, and by extension consumers, on a grand scale. Some of the most common mills are:

- Those who routinely inflate bills
- Those who double dip by overcharging and double charging
- Those whose operation is phony from the doctor on down, and sometimes the attorney as well

Everyone pays for this crime. Entire clinics have been set up for the purpose of filing false claims. Patients with similar criminal inclinations are often paid to participate. When you know of fraudulent medical claims being filed, report it. Otherwise, that nice, new building that won't take your insurance may take cash from someone desperate for medical treatment, then provide him fraudulent services. Most places won't do this because it ratchets them up into the far more serious crime of treating patients without a license. Yet some have gone so far as to do this, and when the heat gets to be too much, they pack up and move to another location.

The Private Investigator will often go undercover as a patient or even employee of these physicians. In this way, she can obtain first-hand information to which she can testify. Surveillance of patients is also an option. Sometimes they can be convinced to testify against the physician or his billing staff in return for immunity from prosecution. This is a tricky situation, however, and must be handled carefully.

5) Product Liability and Wrongful Injury

This type of investigation places you, the investigator, on one side of a claim against the manufacturer and (usually) the seller of an alleged defective product. Investigators who do this work are normally former police detectives or federal special agents who've been highly trained in the special points of making a case of this type.

6) Accident Investigation

Accident investigation is highly specialized, and it is usually performed by PIs who are former law enforcement officials. However, this doesn't mean that you can't intern with one of these people or that an insurance company won't hire you to do so. Do your homework about this and be prepared to show yourself and excellent candidate for further training.

In accident investigation, the Private Investigator learns to use software and hardware to calculate speed and distance travelled before an auto accident. He will learn to determine at what point a driver applied that brakes or if they were applied by measuring any available skid marks on the road at an accident scene. Many other skills are necessary to adequately determine fault in a vehicle accident. This is not limited to vehicular acicular accident, but a Private Investigator will be hired to investigate these most often.

There are also emergency numbers displayed on the hoardings of the Highways were all the accidents are reported and also at the traffic police control room, a Private Investigator can contact them and collect the information along with the footage if available.

7) Corporate Need Investigators

Businesses are required by government regulation to carry workers' compensation insurance. The insurance compensates employees who have sustained on-the-job diseases or injuries with partial wage replacement and full payment of medical and rehabilitation expenses. These are delicate investigations. The employer has an obligation to care for any employee whose injuries result from his employment. Because of this, the employer must treat the claimant as a valued employment. Because of this, the employer must treat the claimant as a valued employee unless this is proven otherwise. Disabled or injured workers deserve compensation. Yet when suspicion is raised, owners must investigate for the sake of the company's fiscal health. Some have such a serious problem with fraud that they spot check all claimants.

Workers' compensation investigations are extremely specialized. The investigator must be familiar with techniques and possess equipment specific to the solving of these cases. The PI must also be familiar with appropriate laws and statutes. For more information, see this site for workers' compensation law by individual state.

If you specialize in workers' compensation, you work for the insurance company. However, never allow yourself to be pressured into looking for an outcome that favours your client. Remain objective in order to be fair to the claimant as well as the employer. Report the facts, no matter what they are and whom they favour.

8) Investigative Options

When workers' comp fraud is suspected, several options are available for determining whether fraud is being committed or not. Some of these options are:

Records check. It's doubtful that a claimant will work where she'll be required to pay taxes, but you might find that she has applied for a loan using her under-the-table workplace or has used that address for some other reason, such as to receive packages.

Activity check. Usually a short surveillance, a day or two, of the claimant's activities. If suspicious behaviour is discovered, a longer surveillance is usually authorized. Sometimes activity checks are ordered when claimants attend doctor's visits, and investigators film activity before and after the visit.

Extended surveillance. Usually ordered as a result of something suspicious uncovered during an activity check and used to determine if it's a pattern of behaviour or a one-time act.

Hidden camera surveillance. When a claimant has very little outside activity, hidden cameras are an answer and can be set up for filming activity when it occurs; an investigator might need to sit for day and even weeks before this person exits the residence.

Private Investigators new to the profession are often appalled at the behaviour of some claimants, but they quickly become numb to the infractions they see.

Private investigators who specialize in workers' compensation investigations will often be asked to provide photographic or video evidence.

9) Interviewing and Interrogation

Information is the business of the private investigator, and information is most often in the hands of people. For the PI, learning how to get the information you need from people is one of the most important parts of your business. Therefore, learning the techniques of interviewing and interrogation is key to success. Obtaining interviews as possible will prevent loss of information, and knowing how to interview a subject will ensure you will get the answers you are looking for.

To Interview or Interrogate-Know the Difference

Interview and interrogations are two very different things. Suspects are interrogated; witnesses are interviewed. Everything that follows can be applied to all types of investigations. However, because of privacy laws, these are certain things the PI may not ask during a pre-employment screening interview.

- Age
- Children and how many times married
- Disability
- Ethnicity
- Marital status
- Political party
- Religion
- Sexual orientation

10) Acknowledging Differences in Perception

When interviewing witnesses, remember that men and women differ in what they remember. This is a generalization, but on that has proven true for the majority. Women look at eyes in an attempt to determine an offender's intent, so they often remember the eyes and at least part of the face.

Experts have written that, contrary to popular opinion, children can be the best witnesses. As with everything else, this is a generalization. Not all children will be good witnesses any more than all women will remember eyes and faces. When properly interviewed, children can give telling aspects of most situations. Of course, age and maturity make a difference.

The most important aspect of interviewing children as witnesses is for the child's recall to be protected. Only an investigator who is trained in interviewing children should ask the child questions or show him pictures. Most experts agree that very young children shouldn't be asked specific questions but should be allowed to speak about the incident in their own time. This very sensitive area has been the subject of books, articles and seminars.

11) Asking Questions Successfully

Never ask a question that suggests the answer. Avoid closed-ended questions, or questions that can be answered with a simple yes or no---- this is the best way to halt an interview. Is an elaboration, providing information that can lead to more questions.

Many investigators begin with questions they already know the answers to. Questions the subject will almost certainly answer truthfully are asked first. This is along the lines of the lie detector question formatting, when a baseline of truthful answers is obtained at the outset. While the investigator doesn't have the subject hooked up to a lie detector, she can watch the subject's mannerisms and judge them against any future answers. This way, she can see how the subject's body responds when he answers a truthful question.

Interviewing Witnesses and Interrogating Suspects

It is vital that you interview both witnesses and suspects to get a clear picture of your case. Interviews and interrogations are handled differently, and it is helpful to know what to expect.

Witnesses

Witnesses are people who have information. They can testify that they've seen, heard, felt, tasted, or touched something that has importance for an investigation.

If the witness is injured and has been taken to the hospital, or must leave the scene for some reason, always ask for her identification and contact information. Be sure to record it from a driver's license or official papers, as some may give false information. Although their percentage is small, some people are afraid to get involved in someone else's accident or incident, and others don't want to.

Be sure to record the license number of your witness vehicle if he has one. The Private Investigator is often in the unfortunate position of interviewing witnesses after the fact because police have gotten to them first. It's not unusual for witnesses to be irritated at the request for further interviews. Yet it's vital that you interview witnesses as soon as possible before their memories start to fade.

In old cases, also known as cold cases, interviewing becomes much more difficult. Witnesses may have had second thoughts or may have been coerced or intimidated by the suspect or those close to him. Witnesses move, change their names, and even die.

Suspects

Interrogation is not merely questioning; it goes beyond questioning and seeks an connecting response from someone who is considered a suspect.Law enforcement officers must inform the suspect's attorney of the time and date of an interrogation and allow him reasonable time to arrive. Witnesses should be present so that there is no question about coercion of the suspect. A typist is usually present as well.

Taking Statements

Cases are won or buried on the strength of statements. Be very sure that you learn to do this most important part of the investigation. On the practical side, be sure that your audio or video equipment works. Take several pens in case one doesn't work, and prepare your questions ahead of time.

Statements can be taken from witnesses or defendants. If taking statements at the behest of an attorney, you'll usually do so in the court recorder's office and all will be taken down. Alternatively, one can take secretary or another investigator with a laptop to type the statement as it's being recorded. Recording of statement is a must. Everyone makes mistakes, especially in early work. Yet a recording protects you from witnesses or defendants who decide to change their minds, who blame you for leading them in a certain direction, or who cry coercion or any other defense a good attorney can dream up.

When you take statements, remember that you're neither defense nor prosecution. No matter which side hires you, you're not trying to prove either side's point. The moment you begin to elicit information that leans toward a conclusion for either side, you've compromised your finest tool objectivity. You are an information gatherer. Let the attorneys slug it out using that information.

Most Private Investigators use audio to record statements, but if you want to be able to go back and study the subject's reaction to your questions, use video to record the statement. Should the case end up in court, video allows these reactions to be visible to the jury as well. The following information should be included at the beginning of any statement you take:

- State the date, time, day, and place
- State your name, occupation, and name of your agency
- Name everyone in the room, an attorney, another investigator, police, court recorder, the fewer people in your interview, the better
- Ask the subject to speak her full name
- Ask the subject to speak her address
- Ask the subject to speak her phone number

- Ask the subject to speak about her identification number/details.
- Ask the subject to speak her occupation and name an place of employment.

Obtaining Confessions

Confessions should be attempted either in threatening note to start with, slowly coming to pleasant way. The fear of threats and physical hardships with advantage of coaxing does help one to give up faster. The repercussions of revealing the facts may incite the subject to come out and be more vocal.

Paranoid Suspects

Sometimes, offenders become so paranoid that they must find out what the police or investigators know. It's not unusual for them to report as witnesses about the very crime they want to find out what information is already known concerning the crime; second, they attempt to provide false information they believe will take the investigation in a different direction; and third, they hope their presence as a witness will keep the investigation away from them.

Sometime, offenders are fascinated by the fact that they're the star of it all. It's all about them, and they delight in their secret knowledge. Many of these won't be able to keep it secret, however; they long for the spotlight and will often make mistakes that result in arrest. At this point, the entire world knows who they are and what they were able to do. Sometimes, they'll even talk if it serves their purpose of gaining stardom. Others toy with investigators, enjoying their sense of power over the authorities.

12) Summary of Financial Needs

Budget your financial start-up needs. This involves pricing everything you'll need, from paper clips to surveillance equipment to furniture. It takes time, but is the only way to ensure that you'll have enough money to generate the healthiest possible start. Include monthly expenses as the beginnings of your budget, and add at least six months operation costs to provide a cushion.

Projections of Earnings and Investor Returns

Provide a description of how you'll return any investor earnings. Work with an accountant to ensure accuracy and feasibility.

Target Market Description

Specialists recommend that new owners identify and focus on the prospective client who possesses the highest potential for monetary return as the target market. This doesn't mean that your market should be entirely limited to this client group, but resources spent gaining these clients are likely to be retuned along with profit. This long-held theory has undergone some criticism in recent years, however. One reason is that many investigators insist that they can't compete in today's market by putting most of their eggs in the target market's basket. They prefer to offer a large menu of services to a larger market. They believe clients expect it. You must decide which theory is best for you.

13) Comparison of Company Services to Competitor Services

Describe your competition's products and services in detail. In what way are you better than your competition? How do you do your specialty better than anyone else? Why would a client choose you rather than the competition? Can you discover areas for improvement; if so, how will you implement improvements?

Marketing and Sales

Start-ups tend to under-price the competition. This is not a good idea. Don't spend time gathering clients whose only concern is low prices when you must eventually raise yours to stay in business. When you raise them, you'll have to go after new clients who will pay your new prices.

Don't undervalue your worth. Perception is key. Don't tell the world that you aren't worth the price everyone else charges. Of course, if a few agencies hold a monopoly in your area and have priced their services egregiously high according to areas with more competition, you may want to rethink this issue.

14) Advertising Venues

Advertising is a large part of your business plan. This is the section in which you indicate the type of advertising you intend to use. Describe the medium in which you'll advertise, how much it will cost, and how you'll pay for it. If you want to increase advertising as you grow, specify how and when.

Work Place-Home Office Versus Public Office

Successful PI firms use many different location models. There is no one right or best model, so choose the one that's right for you viz. home, public, or virtual office.

Home Office

Benefits abound for those who enjoy working from home. Low overhead and tax benefits allow the investigator to retain more profit while finding time to be closer to family. Many who work from home boast of doing some of their work in pyjamas. The Small Business Administration reports a record number of business owners working from home, along with employees of larger businesses.

You can establish office resources you need wherever you feel most comfortable. One can dedicate a room in own home or better dedicate an almirah for safe stowage of equipment, devices and evidences with the proceeding documents and tasking sheets.

Your home is an inconvenient place for meeting clients and lacks the professional atmosphere of an office. Besides, some clients will not be as fond of your children and pets as you are. A distinct disadvantage of the home office is distraction.

Everywhere the business owner looks, he's reminded that he's also the homeowner. A pile of laundry screams for attention, neighbours and delivery people ring the bell. If he has children, interruptions can be constant.

If you work from home, never allow clients access to your address and phone number, and don't make private information publicly available. While most clients are everyday people, this profession will eventually draw the crazy, the frenzied, or the person working off of his last nerve and perhaps his last brain cell. Domestic cases particularly may bring you in contact with this person. Protect yourself and your family.

Public Office

Locating your public office may take some research. If you have very little start-up capital, you may decide to offer investigative work to an attorney or another owner whose business is compatible with yours, with the qualification that you be allowed to use part of his space. Investigators have gotten started this way; however, you must be sure that a written, signed agreement outlines the responsibilities of both parties. Include the number and type of work hours required for your use of space. Otherwise, the agreement can become confusing.

Before deciding on your public location, return to your business plan and the demographics of your target market. If you don't intend to specialize, this may not matter, but if you plan to work with attorneys, for example, look at their income, age, and lifestyle before determining your location. Be sure that you'll be in the right place to attract and service them. Attorney's offices tend to cluster in or near urban areas because of the proximity to courthouses, police departments, jails, and centres for records. Yet this depends on the type of law the attorneys practice. You may also find them in small commercial and even residential areas.

Before locating your public office, be sure that the population of your target market is adequate to support to support your business, or is at least large enough for profitable specialization. Equally important is the need for a stable or rising area economic base. Don't get stuck with a lease that traps you in an area where businesses are floundering or dying.

Virtual Office

Virtual offices are fairly new arrivals on the scene. A virtual office isn't physical space. The purpose is to provide everything the business owner needs while saving the costs of space. This allows the small business owner to be based at home or in an inexpensive space but still show an upscale address to his clients. Services can be added according to the owner's budget or preferences, but the basic virtual office is an address in a prestigious area, with mail receipt and forwarding, discounts on supplies and couriers, and low-priced leasing of offices and meeting rooms for short periods of time. Other features, such as a telephone receptionist, a fax and phone redirection service, and more, can be added. While you work affordably from home, on one will ever know, because you schedule meetings in this sumptuous conference room.

Somewhat on the order of executive suites, virtual offices are set up to fit the needs of those who cannot or will not expend the cost of regular office space. Executive suites provide short-term leases complete with a telephone and receptionist, common area privileges (bathroom, kitchen, conference room), and mail service. Copy/fax machines and other services are available for a fee. Executive suites are attractive to those who require services sporadically, paying only for what they need when they need it.

Automate Office by Virtual Assistants

A virtual office assistant works efficiently well as a regular assistant from home. The assistant answers phone, text messages, types reports, and if you want, acts as the face of your business. However, if you only need an assistant for certain hours or certain days, she's there for you. While there will be no office space in which to meet clients, your virtual assistant will provide the image of a better office setting. Many clients do get impressed with this.

15) Office Equipment and Furnishings

Appearing professional and successful need not cost a fortune. Be creative. Depending on available time and motivation, you can find solid wooden pieces at unfinished furniture stores just waiting to be stained and finished. Remember, besides furnishing a nice office, if you seek the high-income client, you must locate where she is. Don't expect this client to meet you in a dingy third-floor walk-up with poor lighting and shabby furniture.

One small aside regarding the use of antiques to furnish your office: As office furniture, they will depreciate, but as antiques, they will grow in value, providing the benefits of tax deductions and increased capital worth in one package.

16) Marketing and Promotion

The purpose of marketing is to ensure that the pricing and packaging of your services and/or products creates demand and makes people eager to purchase from you. Advertising today is very different than it was as recently as ten years ago. Hashtags has led to more specific kind of advertising. Social media platforms also offer great opportunities.

Animated gifs, images, are also considered a great attraction to get the potential client. The secret to connecting with people even strangerslies in asking questions. Let the other speak, and respond with appropriate questions reflecting your interest in what they've said.

Advertisement for Branding

There is a remarkable difference in advertising for branding and advertising for sales. As evident, branding focuses on the company while the sales is more oriented on marketing of the services

Many people will advise you never to put money into a logo that will need to be updated later at additional cost. If you have the funds to have your logo professionally created at start up. It's pricey to do so, and all companies update them periodically to show a fresh new look. This leads to the other school of thought: Lacking the means to do anything else, create your own logo, or have it done with minimal cost in order to get your business up and running. Of course, if you have no talent for this, don't do it yourself. You know if something looks professional; if you can't create this look, forget it.

A professional looking business card is considered highly necessary for developing contacts and brand recognition. Handouts, leaflets and brochures could be considered as and when the business grows.

One can even have some promotional materials like pens, pocket calendars or key chains, etc with your name and logo, with other contact details.

Networking

Many networking groups meet frequently. The networking group may be of different business orientation, but a private investigator can fit in any type of investigation in any business module. Some meetings are paid though, but can be very useful to the investigator to develop networking. One should not try to visualise where work is or client is likely, the work and client-age would flow automatically.

Carry enough business cards, for more liberal distribution. Remember, no one wants to express others that they need a private investigator for some investigation, but the fact remains that almost all would like to be associated with the private investigator for some work or the other.

17) Creating a Website

No marketing tool is more recommended than a business Website. You may still want to use the Yellow Pages or something like it, but do not neglect securing a presence on the Web. When asked, many business owners report searching the Web first for products and services, and many never reference the phone book at all. If you know nothing about using the Internet, now is a good time to learn. Colleges offer low-cost community programs that teach computer and Internet basics. Online programs are also available, as well as educational software.

Website Basics

If your aversion to learning this technology is strong, you can pay someone to create, maintain, and operate your site. If you do, set up some means of employee oversight to be sure you haven't put a shyster in charge of the house; do a background check for past reported offenses. If you can budget the funds, hire a good Web site designer who has a track record with other businesses. Unfortunately, whenever there's a demand for any service, fraudulent and incompetent companies spring up to fill it like toadstools after rain. Many will like to advertise that they design a great site. Be sure to check them out before deciding on one.

It is important to note here that any query coming through your website should be received on your email. A professional looking email is advisable.

When you look at different developers, make a list of characteristics you'd like your site to have. Ask each candidate to supply a portfolio of links to live sites they have designed. Go to each site and note whether the designs look professional and the sites are easy to navigate. Be sure that your designer doesn't crowd Web pages with too much text bunched up in one long paragraph. Breaking text up with space and pictures makes it more attractive and readable. Be careful with inexperienced designers, but don't write them off immediately. They may be able to give you a great Web site for a low price; just ask to see examples of other projects and be very detailed with your questions.

After you choose your designer, obtain a written contract of exactly what has been agreed upon with regards to the format, number of pages, and any flash or specialty features. To avoid being duped, require a breakdown of costs that can be readily understood. Put charges and fees in writing as well. Communicating by e-mail provides a record of your transactions from the outset. If you intend to create login pages, be aware of the necessity of encrypting your passwords, or else anyone can easily login by a hacking methodology called sql injections.

Publishing your site doesn't guarantee that anyone will ever see it. Once it's operational, you must inform the world that it exists. You must drive business to your site with effective marketing.

If you have less money than time, you can put together a simple but effective Web site yourself. Many companies host do-it-yourself sites and provide support. Prices vary, so search thoroughly before deciding on your host.

Ready-made or template sites such as these don't offer the flexibility that custom-built sites provide. However, for the price and limited time required to launch them, ready-made sites are functional and attractive. Flash and special features can also be added. When you choose a site, decide which features you absolutely must have, then work with that list and your budget to find the right hosting company.

Marketing Your Website

If you do an Internet search for Web site marketing, you'll find a lot of information on one important marketing tool: search engine optimization, a method for having your site appear higher on an Internet searcher's key word search results page. In other works, when a client enters a search for "private investigators your city, your state" into any search engine, many pages will be returned. You don't want your site to be listed on page fifty, as most people don't search past page three. Optimization can improve your standing on the list. However, don't believe any claims that guarantee you'll appear on the first page or within the first ten sites returned. In the advancing digital technology, no one can guarantee this. One can use the hash tags to get more mileage of any webpage. Many use search engine optimisation (SEO) to get ranked higher in the search engine.

18) Creating Professional Reports

The final report is as important as any other part of your investigation. It must appear professional and informative. All your efforts won't matter much to your client. People are influenced by what they see, and a professionally typed and formatted report that is easy to read and free of any spelling or grammatical mistakes will add credibility to your investigation and its results. To some degree, this may be simple perception. The ability to write a good report may, in reality, not reflect on your investigative skills, but only you will be aware of that. A report has several sections: title page, introduction, body, conclusion, and additional information.

Remember that this is highly sensitive information concerning another person. Because you're responsible for keeping this confidential, store it in a safe location. Most investigators lock their case files and evidences. Take special measures not to leak the investigative approach and the findings.

Body of Report

This can be written in several formats. Some investigators write the report as a day-by-day recounting of the events, many times in paragraph form. The format that seems to be most readable is that of incident-by-incident reporting. In other words, the top of the page shows the day and date. The highlights of the day are reported in first-person or third-person narrative.

October 27, 2008

6:00 A.M. Investigator left his residence.

6:30 A.M Arrived at target residence and set up surveillance.

7:00 A.M Ms. XYZ exited residence with two children.

Conclusion

At the end of this report, summary ofthe findings vis-à-vis objective achieved will need to be enlisted in paragraphs. Any recommendations can be included here. This has to be precise indicating the objective achieved.

List of Additional Information

In this section, you'll add any sketches, pictures, itemization and location of DVDs, interviews or background check information, official records, and the like.

Polishing the Report

The report must be in a template type with details of the information provided and obtained after investigations. Emphasis should be on the correct use of grammar and spellings.

Appendix A

Cheating Case

CHEATING CASE

To be filled by the PI/applicant and signed

FORM NO. :

APPLICANT INFORMATION		
FIRST	LAST NAME	DOB
ADDRESS		FLAT/QTR
CITY	STATE	PIN
APPLICANT'S MOBILE	APPLICANT'S E-MAIL	
NAME/SUBJECT	RELATION & CONTACT DETAILS OF SUBJECT'S PARAMOUR	
SUBJECT'S DETAILS IMPORTANT INPUTS		
CONTACT DETAILS (MOBILE & EMAIL):		

HOBBIES/WEAKNESS	
OBJECTIVE: (TASK)	

PASTE PP SIZE PHOTOGRAPH OF SUSPECT HERE

SOCIAL MEDIA ACCOUNT DETAILS (IF KNOWN)
LINKEDIN PROFILE (IF ANY):
FACEBOOK PROFILE (IF ANY):
TWITTER PROFILE (IF ANY):

TERMS & CONDITIONS WITH SIGNATURE

I understand that I will disclose all facts and not give my opinion

I certify that my statement recorded above are true and complete to the best of my knowledge and that false or misleading information in my request will be my responsibility for any legal/embarrassing consequences.

I hereby authorize the Private Investigator to undertake fact finding investigation and agree to the cost of undertaking the investigation as intimated by him. I also understand my request for this fact finding is only for the Private Investigator and am fully responsible for initiating such investigation on my own.

FULL NAME /SIGN OF APPLICANT	**Date & Time**

IMPORTANT NOTES FOR PRIVATE INESTIGATOR:

ENDORSING DATE & TIME AND SENDING IT BY EMAIL WILL MEAN ACCEPTANCE OF TERMS BY THE APPLICANT

CHECK LIST TO be suspicious when your spouse: Answer if relevant

- ☐ Has a new interest in exercise and losing weight (5 marks)
- ☐ Buys you gifts without reason (5 marks)
- ☐ Tells you the boss wants him or her to work a lot of over time on a "special" project (10 marks)
- ☐ Suddenly buys a SIM or communicating device (5 marks)
- ☐ Starts spending more time on mobile messengers (5 marks)
- ☐ Closes his room & talks with somebody on pretext of getting disturbed while talking with client. (10 marks)
- ☐ Starts spending more time alone behind closed doors. (10 marks)
- ☐ Expresses little interest in sex (5 marks)
- ☐ Expresses more interest in sex (5 marks)
- ☐ Expresses interest in new sexual techniques (5 marks)
- ☐ Begins to dress differently (5 marks)
- ☐ Hides or purchases new fragrances or lingerie (5 marks)
- ☐ Begins taking longer and more business trips (10 marks)
- ☐ Has a new circle of friends (5 marks)
- ☐ Comes home smelling of alcohol or perfume (10 marks)
- ☐ Begins to leave for work early (10 marks)
- ☐ Shows little or atypical interest in family matters (5 marks)
- ☐ Makes several unexplained credit/debit card purchases (10 marks)
- ☐ Begins to talk about wanting more "space" from you (10 marks)
- ☐ Is caught not wearing a wedding ring (10 marks)
- ☐ Has excessive and unexplained mileage on the car (5 marks)
- ☐ Spends an inordinate amount of time on the computer (5 marks)
- ☐ Comes home with suspicious stains on clothing (10 marks)
- ☐ Expresses a sudden and unexplained surge of energy (5 marks)
- ☐ Is always late (5 marks)
- ☐ Is overly protective of a briefcase, calendar, address book, organizer, mobiles, and/or computer (5 marks) (10 marks)
- ☐ Expresses a new interest in eating different dishes (5 marks)
- ☐ Begins to buy new clothes (5 marks)
- ☐ Doesn't get signal in mobile for long time and gives quick short calls (5 marks)
- ☐ Gets irritated on getting calls and messages from spouse & talks less (10 marks)
- ☐ Arrives home from work smelling of different soap and a fresh shower (10 marks)

TOTAL SCORE: 220 **OBTAINED SCORE:**

60 <= : SAFE
65 – 80 : DOUBTFUL
80 – 150 : HIGH CHANCES
155 – 200 : CONFIRMED

TASKING: CASE TAKEN/NOT TAKEN

ENDORSING DATE & TIME AND SENDING IT BY EMAIL WILL MEAN ACCEPTANCE OF TERMS BY THE APPLICANT

Appendix B

Divorce, Infidelity and Child Custody Investigations

DIVORCE, INFIDELITY AND CHILD CUSTODY INVESTIGATIONS

To be filled by the PI/applicant and signed

FORM NO. :

APPLICANT INFORMATION		
FIRST	LAST NAME	DOB
ADDRESS		FLAT/QTR
CITY	STATE	PIN
APPLICANT'S MOBILE	APPLICANT'S E-MAIL	
NAME/SUBJECT	RELATION & CONTACT DETAILS OF SUBJECT'S PARAMOUR	
SPOUSE DETAILS **IMPORTANT INPUTS**		
CONTACT DETAILS (MOBILE & EMAIL):		

HOBBIES/WEAKNESS	
OBJECTIVE: (TASK)	

PASTE PP SIZE PHOTOGRAPH OF SUSPECT HERE

SOCIAL MEDIA ACCOUNT DETAILS (IF KNOWN)
LINKEDIN PROFILE (IF ANY):
FACEBOOK PROFILE (IF ANY):
TWITTER PROFILE (IF ANY):

TERMS & CONDITIONS WITH SIGNATURE

I understand that I will disclose all facts and not give my opinion

I certify that my statement recorded above are true and complete to the best of my knowledge and that false or misleading information in my request will be my responsibility for any legal/embarrassing consequences..

I hereby authorize the Private Investigator to undertake fact finding investigation and agree to the cost of undertaking the investigation as intimated by him. I also understand my request for this fact finding is only for the Private Investigator and are fully responsible for initiating such investigation on my own.

FULL NAME / SIGN OF APPLICANT	**Date & Time**

IMPORTANT NOTES FOR PRIVATE INESTIGATOR:

ENDORSING DATE & TIME AND SENDING IT BY EMAIL WILL MEAN ACCEPTANCE OF TERMS BY THE APPLICANT

QUESTIONAIRE LIST TO CASE (Cheating check list in Appendix A, if relevant)

- ☐ Do you suspect any other partner in your spouse life? If yes, please give details with address and contact nos.__________
- ☐ How many children do you have, give details of their age, sex and attached to dad or mom?
  - o __________
- ☐ Are you seeking alimony? __________
- ☐ Have you left on your own or have you been sent out?__________
- ☐ Is any of your valuable with your spouse? Details__________
- ☐ Any evidence of domestic violence or medical of injury or photo?__________
  - o __________
- ☐ Details of sex life __________
- ☐ Parents/Inlaws involvement __________
- ☐ Which all bank accounts does your partner have?__________
- ☐ Details of any previous complaint __________
- ☐ Details of the applicant's lawyer __________
- ☐ Details of the opponent's lawyer __________
- ☐ Does the applicant know the whereabout of the spouse?__________
- ☐ Who has the ownership of the SIM card of the applicant's SIM and spouse SIM?_____
- ☐ __________
- ☐ Knowledge of the spouse in IT:__________
- ☐ How many Debit Card or Credit Cards does your spouse have?__________
- ☐ Does he give money after seperation? Did you ask for money?__________
- ☐ Your spouse office details and property details__________
- ☐ __________

Any additional information about the spouse:

Objective of the case:

TASKING: CASE TAKEN/NOT TAKEN

ENDORSING DATE & TIME AND SENDING IT BY EMAIL WILL MEAN ACCEPTANCE OF TERMS BY THE APPLICANT

Appendix C

Insurance Frauds

INSURANCE FRAUDS

To be filled by the PI/applicant and signed

FORM NO. :

APPLICANT INFORMATION		
FIRST	LAST NAME	DOB
ADDRESS		FLAT/QTR
CITY	STATE	PIN
APPLICANT'S MOBILE	APPLICANT'S E-MAIL	
NAME	CONTACT DETAILS OF INSURANCE AGENTS	
TRANSACTION DETAILS		
CONTACT DETAILS (MOBILE & EMAIL):		

EVIDENCES	
OBJECTIVE: (TASK)	

PASTE PP SIZE PHOTOGRAPH OF SUSPECT HERE

SOCIAL MEDIA ACCOUNT DETAILS (IF KNOWN)
LINKEDIN PROFILE (IF ANY):
FACEBOOK PROFILE (IF ANY):
TWITTER PROFILE (IF ANY):

TERMS & CONDITIONS WITH SIGNATURE

I understand that I will disclose all facts and not give my opinion

I certify that my statement recorded above are true and complete to the best of my knowledge and that false or misleading information in my request will be my responsibility for any legal/embarrassing consequences.

I hereby authorize the Private Investigator to undertake fact finding investigation and agree to the cost of undertaking the investigation as intimated by him. I also understand my request for this fact finding is only for the Private Investigator and am fully responsible for initiating such investigation on my own.

FULL NAME / SIGN OF APPLICANT	**Date & Time**

IMPORTANT NOTES FOR PRIVATE INESTIGATOR:

ENDORSING DATE & TIME AND SENDING IT BY EMAIL WILL MEAN ACCEPTANCE OF TERMS BY THE APPLICANT

QUESTIONAIRE LIST TO INSURANCE FRAUDS

- [ ] Please give details with address, contact nos. and emails of the Insurance Agent/s ______
- [ ] Give details of the Money lost and no. of transactions made in different accounts and from whose accounts the money was sent______
- [ ] Details of any complaint made (Copy required of the complaint/FIR) ______
- [ ] Statement Copy to be given______
- [ ] Details of Money sent from which all accounts ______
- [ ] Did the insurance agent ever meet, if so, when and where?______
- [ ] Details any shared documents, Chats, Emails, Bank Accounts of the fraudsters, id proofs of fraudster and Bank Account details with IFSC codes ______
- [ ] Who referred the Insurance Agents ______
- [ ] Can you recognise the Fraudster/s?______
- [ ] Details of any previous complaint______
- [ ] Any details of the Social Media accounts of the fraudster/s ______
- [ ] When did the fraudster/s pick up your calls last? ______
- [ ] Type of the transactions made (Credit /Debit Card, NEFT, Cash Deposits)?______
- [ ] Details of any duplicate/fake websites links suggested by fraudsters:______
- [ ] ______
- [ ] Did the fraudster ask you to download any mobile application stating that the relationship manager will guide?______
- [ ] Have you taken any loan to pay the amount?______
- [ ] Did you try to speak to any Insurance Company's representative? Give details ______
- [ ] Did you receive any email or message from the Insurance Company regarding the initial policy or activation of policy? Give details ______
- [ ] ______

Any additional information about the incident:

Objective of the case:

TASKING: CASE TAKEN/NOT TAKEN

ENDORSING DATE & TIME AND SENDING IT BY EMAIL WILL MEAN ACCEPTANCE OF TERMS BY THE APPLICANT

Appendix D

Accident Investigations

ACCIDENT INVESTIGATIONS

To be filled by the PI/applicant and signed

FORM NO. :

APPLICANT INFORMATION		
FIRST	LAST NAME	DOB
ADDRESS		FLAT/QTR
CITY	STATE	PIN
APPLICANT'S MOBILE	APPLICANT'S E-MAIL	
NAME	CONTACT DETAILS OF INSURANCE AGENTS	
ACCIDENT DETAILS		
CONTACT DETAILS (MOBILE & EMAIL):		

EVIDENCES	
OBJECTIVE: (TASK)	

PASTE PP SIZE PHOTOGRAPH OF SUSPECT HERE	SOCIAL MEDIA ACCOUNT DETAILS (IF KNOWN) LINKEDIN PROFILE (IF ANY): FACEBOOK PROFILE (IF ANY): TWITTER PROFILE (IF ANY):

TERMS & CONDITIONS WITH SIGNATURE

I understand that I will disclose all facts and not give my opinion

I certify that my statement recorded above are true and complete to the best of my knowledge and that false or misleading information in my request will be my responsibility for any legal/embarrassing consequences.

I hereby authorize the Private Investigator to undertake fact finding investigation and agree to the cost of undertaking the investigation as intimated by him. I also understand my request for this fact finding is only for the Private Investigator and am fully responsible for initiating such investigation on my own.

FULL NAME / SIGN OF APPLICANT	Date & Time

IMPORTANT NOTES FOR PRIVATE INESTIGATOR:

ENDORSING DATE & TIME AND SENDING IT BY EMAIL WILL MEAN ACCEPTANCE OF TERMS BY THE APPLICANT

QUESTIONAIRE LIST TO ACCIDENT INVESTIGATIONS

- ☐ Do you recognize actual accident site? Give details: (Applicant may have to show the accident site) ____________
- ☐ Explain your version of accident: ____________
- ☐ Details of any complaint made (Copy required of the complaint/FIR) ____________
- ☐ Vehicle used by your relative/friend ____________
- ☐ Details of vehicle used by the other party ____________
- ☐ Details of the opponent driver (Name, age, address, contact details) ____________
  - o ____________
- ☐ Hospital where your relative was taken immediately after accident and by whom? ____________
  - o ____________
- ☐ Life Insurance Agents' details of both the parties (if any) ____________
  - o ____________
- ☐ Details of both the parties medical first aid fees/charge/s ____________
  - o ____________
- ☐ Vehicle Insurance Details of both the parties ____________
- ☐ Vehicle repair charges of both the parities: ____________
  - o ____________
- ☐ Did any death take place: (Give details): ____________
  - o ____________
- ☐ Do you any details of eye witness? ____________
- ☐ ____________
- ☐ ____________
- ☐ Did any bystander help the accident victims? (Give details) ____________
  - o ____________
- ☐ Was any driver or victim in the influence of liqour? ____________
- ☐ How many people were injured during the accident? ____________
  - o ____________
- ☐ Job/professional details of other party members/relatives. Give details ____________
  - o ____________
- ☐ ____________

Any additional information about the incident:

Objective of the case:

TASKING: CASE TAKEN/NOT TAKEN

ENDORSING DATE & TIME AND SENDING IT BY EMAIL WILL MEAN ACCEPTANCE OF TERMS BY THE APPLICANT

Appendix E

Murder/Suicide Investigations

MURDER/SUICIDE INVESTIGATIONS

To be filled by the applicant and signed

FORM NO. :

APPLICANT INFORMATION		
FIRST	LAST NAME	DOB
ADDRESS		FLAT/QTR
CITY	STATE	PIN
APPLICANT'S MOBILE	APPLICANT'S E-MAIL	
NAME	CONTACT DETAILS OF INSURANCE AGENTS	
DECEASED DETAILS		
CONTACT DETAILS (MOBILE & EMAIL):		

EVIDENCES	
OBJECTIVE: (TASK)	

PASTE PP SIZE PHOTOGRAPH OF SUSPECT HERE

SOCIAL MEDIA ACCOUNT DETAILS (IF KNOWN)
LINKEDIN PROFILE (IF ANY):
FACEBOOK PROFILE (IF ANY):
TWITTER PROFILE (IF ANY):

TERMS & CONDITIONS WITH SIGNATURE

I understand that I will disclose all facts and not give my opinion

I certify that my statement recorded above are true and complete to the best of my knowledge and that false or misleading information in my request will be my responsibility for any legal/embarrassing consequences.

I hereby authorize the Private Investigator to undertake fact finding investigation and agree to the cost of undertaking the investigation as intimated by him. I also understand my request for this fact finding is only for the Private Investigator and am fully responsible for initiating such investigation on my own.

FULL NAME /SIGN OF APPLICANT	Date & Time

IMPORTANT NOTES FOR PRIVATE INESTIGATOR:

ENDORSING DATE & TIME AND SENDING IT BY EMAIL WILL MEAN ACCEPTANCE OF TERMS BY THE APPLICANT

QUESTIONAIRE LIST TO MURDER/SUICIDE INVESTIGATIONS

- ☐ How are you related to the deceased? Give details: (Applicant may have to explain if immediate relative is not the applicant) ____________
- ☐ Explain your version of death: ____________
- ☐ Details of any complaint made (Copy required of the complaint/FIR) ____________
- ☐ Was is a normal death or doubtful? ____________
- ☐ Details of post mortem if any ____________
- ☐ Details of his/her friends (Name, age, address, contact details) ____________
  - o ____________
- ☐ Hospital where the deceased was taken and was his dying statement taken? ____________
  - o ____________
- ☐ Who has benefitted after his/her death (financially/property wise) ____________
  - o ____________
- ☐ Was the deceased suffering with any illness and who was/has been treating him/her ____________
  - o ____________
- ☐ How many years since marriage ____________
- ☐ How was the relationship with spouse: ____________
  - o ____________
- ☐ Details of friends of the spouse: ____________
  - o ____________
- ☐ Do you any details of wifi routers around? (SSID of both the parties) ____________
- ☐ ____________
- ☐ ____________
- ☐ Do you have the CDR of his/her mobiles? (Give details) ____________
  - o ____________
- ☐ Do you have his PC/Laptop password? His mobile screen lock passeword or email/fb/whatsapp details? ____________
- ☐ Details of the best friend of the deceased and spouse? ____________
  - o ____________
- ☐ Did the person have any criminal required? Give details ____________
  - o ____________
- ☐ Was he/she involved in any polygamy or extra marital affairs? Give details of spouse suspicions ____________

Any additional information about the incident:

Objective of the case:

TASKING: CASE TAKEN/NOT TAKEN

ENDORSING DATE & TIME AND SENDING IT BY EMAIL WILL MEAN ACCEPTANCE OF TERMS BY THE APPLICANT

Appendix F

Missing/Absconding Person's Investigations

MISSING/ABSCONDING PERSONS' INVESTIGATIONS

To be filled by the applicant and signed

FORM NO. :

APPLICANT INFORMATION		
FIRST	LAST NAME	DOB
ADDRESS		FLAT/QTR
CITY	STATE	PIN
APPLICANT'S MOBILE	APPLICANT'S E-MAIL	
DOB/MISSING PERSON	NAME OF MISSING PERSON & MISSING SINCE:	
MISSING PERSON'S DETAILS	PHYSICAL, LAST CLOTHES WHEN LEFT HOUSE	
CONTACT DETAILS (MOBILE & EMAIL):		

EVIDENCES	
OBJECTIVE: (TASK)	

PASTE PP SIZE PHOTOGRAPH OF SUSPECT HERE	SOCIAL MEDIA ACCOUNT DETAILS (IF KNOWN) LINKEDIN PROFILE (IF ANY): FACEBOOK PROFILE (IF ANY): TWITTER PROFILE (IF ANY):

TERMS & CONDITIONS WITH SIGNATURE

I understand that I will disclose all facts and not give my opinion

I certify that my statement recorded above are true and complete to the best of my knowledge and that false or misleading information in my request will be my responsibility for any legal/embarrassing consequences.

I hereby authorize the Private Investigator to undertake fact finding investigation and agree to the cost of undertaking the investigation as intimated by him. I also understand my request for this fact finding is only for the Private Investigator and am fully responsible for initiating such investigation on my own.

FULL NAME /SIGN OF APPLICANT	**Date & Time**

IMPORTANT NOTES FOR PRIVATE INESTIGATOR:

ENDORSING DATE & TIME AND SENDING IT BY EMAIL WILL MEAN ACCEPTANCE OF TERMS BY THE APPLICANT

QUESTIONAIRE LIST TO MISSING/ABSCONDING PERSON'S INVESTIGATION

- ☐ How are you related to the missing person? Give details: (Applicant may have to explain if immediate relative is not the applicant) ____________
  - o ____________
- ☐ Suspicion if any, on the reason of missing/absconding. ____________
  - o ____________
- ☐ Details of any complaint made (Copy required of the complaint/FIR) ____________
- ☐ Was any family dispute or any affair/adultery ____________
- ☐ Details of all his bank accounts and ATM/Credit cards, if any ____________
  - o ____________
- ☐ Details of his/her friends (Name, age, address, contact details) ____________
  - o ____________
- ☐ Details of illness/treatment being taken in immediate past? ____________
  - o ____________
- ☐ Details of money (cash) or jewelry is missing? ____________
  - o ____________
- ☐ Was the person suffering with any depression? ____________
  - o ____________
- ☐ Is the missing/absconding person married? Since when? ____________
  - o ____________
- ☐ How was the relationship with spouse/friend/fb/gf: ____________
  - o ____________
  - o ____________
- ☐ Details of friends of the person: ____________
  - o ____________
- ☐ Describe last few days of his behaviour: ____________
- ☐ ____________
- ☐ ____________
- ☐ Do you have the CDR of his/her mobiles? (Give details) ____________
  - o ____________
- ☐ Do you have his PC/Laptop password? His mobile screen lock passeword or email/fb/whatsapp details? ____________
- ☐ Details of any loan pending? ____________
- ☐ Did the person have any criminal record? Give details ____________
  - o ____________
- ☐ Explain his/her hobbies. ____________

Any additional information about the incident:

Objective of the case:

TASKING: CASE TAKEN/ NOT TAKEN

ENDORSING DATE & TIME AND SENDING IT BY EMAIL WILL MEAN ACCEPTANCE OF TERMS BY THE APPLICANT

Appendix G

Spouse/Child's Social Media Activity Investigations

SPOUSE/CHILD'S SOCIAL MEDIA ACTIVITY INVESTIGATIONS

To be filled by the applicant and signed

FORM NO. : G/

APPLICANT INFORMATION		
FIRST	LAST NAME	DOB
ADDRESS		FLAT/QTR
CITY	STATE	PIN
APPLICANT'S MOBILE	APPLICANT'S E-MAIL	
DOB/CHILD/SPOUSE	NAME OF CHILD/SPOUSE:	
CHILD/SPOUSE ACTIVITY DETAILS		
CONTACT DETAILS (MOBILE & EMAIL):		

EVIDENCES	
OBJECTIVE: (TASK)	

PASTE PP SIZE PHOTOGRAPH OF SUSPECT HERE

SOCIAL MEDIA ACCOUNT DETAILS (IF KNOWN)
LINKEDIN PROFILE (IF ANY):
FACEBOOK PROFILE (IF ANY):
TWITTER PROFILE (IF ANY):

TERMS & CONDITIONS WITH SIGNATURE

I understand that I will disclose all facts and not give my opinion

I certify that my statement recorded above are true and complete to the best of my knowledge and that false or misleading information in my request will be my responsibility for any legal/embarrassing consequences.

I hereby authorize the Private Investigator to undertake fact finding investigation and agree to the cost of undertaking the investigation as intimated by him. I also understand my request for this fact finding is only for the Private Investigator and am fully responsible for initiating such investigation on my own.

FULL NAME /SIGN OF APPLICANT	**Date & Time**

IMPORTANT NOTES FOR PRIVATE INESTIGATOR:

ENDORSING DATE & TIME AND SENDING IT BY EMAIL WILL MEAN ACCEPTANCE OF TERMS BY THE APPLICANT

SPOUSE/CHILD'S SOCIAL MEDIA ACTIVITY INVESTIGATION

- ☐ Give details of suspicions: ______________________
  - o ______________________
- ☐ What and when did you notice any message/post/activity? ______________________
  - o ______________________
- ☐ Do you suspect any boy friend/girl friend affair or spouse affair/adultery? Give details.
  ____
- ☐ Is he or she not spending time with you? ______________________
- ☐ Details of his/her best friend/s ______________________
  - o ______________________
- ☐ Details of his/her friends (Name, age, address, contact details) ______________________
  - o ______________________
- ☐ Details of his/her friend you feel is influencing him/her? ______________________
  - o ______________________
- ☐ Details of job/education being pursued by him/her? ______________________
  - o ______________________
- ☐ Was the person suffering with any depression? ______________________
  - o ______________________
- ☐ Is the missing/absconding person married? Since when? ______________________
  - o ______________________
- ☐ How was the relationship with spouse/friend/fb/gf: ______________________
  - o ______________________
  - o ______________________
- ☐ Details of eating habits of the person: ______________________
  - o ______________________
- ☐ Details of sleeping habits of the person: ______________________
- ☐ ______________________
- ☐ Do you have his PC/Laptop password? His mobile screen lock passeword or email/fb/whatsapp details? ______________________
- ☐ Details of any Laptop/PC held? ______________________
- ☐ Explain his/her hobbies. ______________________

Any additional information about the incident:

Objective of the case:

TASKING: CASE TAKEN/ NOT TAKEN

ENDORSING DATE & TIME AND SENDING IT BY EMAIL WILL MEAN ACCEPTANCE OF TERMS BY THE APPLICANT

CYBER CRIME HELPLINE LLP

We undertake technical investigations, cyber forensics and job oriented cyber courses

Head Office

2S2B, KonarkIndrayu Premises,KondhwaRoad, Kondhwa, Pune, Maharashtra

Kondhwa Branch

225B & 226B, KonarkIndrayu Premises,KondhwaRoad, Kondhwa, Pune, Maharashtra

Camp Branch

206, West Wing, Aurora Towers, 9 Molodina Road, Camp, Pune, Maharashtra

https://cybercrimehelpline.in

https://cchclasses.com

https://cybercrimehelp.com

Facebook: https://www.facebook.com/Cyber-Crime-Helpline-LLP

Instagram: https://www.instagram.com/cybercrime_helpline/

Email:cchadvisor@gmail.com, privateinvestigator.cch@gmail.com

Our Guidance is Free

Our Job Oriented Courses

Diploma in Comprehensive Cyber Investigation Course

Certified Private Investigator's Course

Our Skills

Missing/Absconding Persons

Cyber Forensics

Corporate Investigations

Assistance to police on Corporate Investigations